Melissa,

It's been such a great pleasure, both personally and professionally, to work with you. I'm glad you were part of the Settlement Family these four years. May you be blessed with all that makes you happiest in the years to come. Please keep in touch.

Love,
Lori

And They
Shall Have Music

Almeda C. Adams (1865-1949)
Founder of The Cleveland Music School Settlement;
from a portrait by Eileen Ingalls at the Settlement

And They Shall Have Music

The History of The Cleveland Music School Settlement

by

Silvia Zverina

THE COBHAM AND HATHERTON PRESS
CLEVELAND, OHIO
1988

And They Shall Have Music
A History of The Cleveland Music School Settlement
Copyright © 1988 by The Cleveland Music School Settlement

Book design by Roderick Boyd Porter

Photograph of Ingalls portrait of Almeda C. Adams
   by Kevin C. Vesely

First edition

Manufactured in the United States of America

Library of Congress Cataloging-in-Publication Data

Zverina, Silvia, 1903-
   And they shall have music

   Includes index.
   1. Cleveland Music School Settlement.   I. Title.
MT4.C7C7748   1988   780'.7'2977132   87-29914
ISBN 0-944125-06-9

To Justin
whose love and
unflagging interest
made possible
And They Shall Have Music

Foreword

THE INSTIGATOR of this history was Dorothy Humel Hovorka. As president of The Cleveland Music School Settlement during its sixtieth anniversary, she felt that an account of this institution's achievements would be of value. The chief aim has been to be as accurate as possible and to recount the major events. Inevitably, some events may have been inadvertently omitted, and possibly names of trustees, faculty, staff, donors, and others who have aided the Settlement over the years may not have been mentioned. This was not by design, but rather because records in some instances are succinct. It is hoped that the general accomplishments of the School have been made manifest.

The task would not have been possible at all without the interest and cooperation of many people. Thanks should go especially to Dorothy Humel Hovorka, who as honorary trustee and former president of the board, has read and re-read the manuscript, offering both information and valuable suggestions, as well as editorial aid. In addition, the following trustees, both former and present, with special knowledge of the Settlement also read the history to verify information: Mrs. Cyrus Clark Ford, Mrs. Thomas Munro, Alexander C. Robinson III, Paul L. Eden, Richard D. Peters, Dr. Lester G. Glick, and Edward F. Meyers. Past and present faculty and staff members who also provided assistance were: Mr. and Mrs. Hyman Schandler, Miss Margaret Sharp, Howard Whittaker, Gilbert Brooks, and Richard H. Kauffman. Mrs. A. Beverly Barksdale, a member of The Fortnightly Musical Club, researched the records of that organization to clarify the Club's position in the founding of the School.

I am most grateful to all.

Silvia Zverina

Introduction

DURING THE SUMMER of 1972, shortly after assuming the presidency of The Cleveland Music School Settlement, I asked Silvia Zverina, a newly-elected trustee, to write this history. With her educational background, professional experience, and deep interest in the fine arts, Silvia was highly qualified to undertake this task. She readily agreed, but at the time, neither of us fully realized the magnitude of the work required for such a project nor the problems that would be encountered.

Upon learning that the records from 1912 to 1925 were missing, Silvia spent many months in The Cleveland Public Library and The Western Reserve Historical Society Library researching the Settlement's development during these important initial years. After perusing all the local newspapers of that period, she read the forty-seven years of minutes that were available; it was only then that Silvia began the actual writing from her copious notes.

The history was almost complete, when the missing records were found. Although it was gratifying to have all the facts in hand, this discovery necessitated considerable rewriting, after which the history was read by numerous trustees and staff members. They made suggestions for additions and posed questions that required more research, all of which took time. Unfortunately, the publication was to be delayed once again, when Silvia became seriously ill in 1979. The assistance of Jean Froelich and Roderick Boyd Porter in bringing this history to print is inestimable.

Rarely have I witnessed a volunteer with a dedication to an institution as that of Silvia Zverina to The Cleveland Music School Settlement. In addition to the years of work devoted to this history, she and her husband, Justin, are among the most generous donors to the Settlement. Theirs has been an extraordinary contribution. The Zverinas and I hope that this history will inspire others — trustees, administrators, and faculty — to carry on the traditions of service established by the many remarkable people who have been associated with this institution.

Dorothy Humel Hovorka

A note about sources: The resources consulted in the research for *And They Shall Have Music* have been the minutes of the board of trustees (and its various committees) of The Cleveland Music School Settlement; cited editions of the *Cleveland Plain Dealer, The Cleveland Press,* and *Town Topics;* and material in the archives of the Settlement and in the collections of The Cleveland Public Library and The Western Reserve Historical Society.

Table of Contents

1. A Dream Comes True

TIMES CHANGE, CITIES CHANGE. Institutions either adapt to altered circumstances and prosper, or they remain static and may even disappear. This is the story of a Cleveland organization that started in a small way but grew to become the largest and one of the most respected community music schools in the United States. Nineteen hundred and twelve was the year that The Cleveland Music School Settlement began.

To place this event in context, we need to consider briefly the history of Cleveland, the origin of its people, the growth of its industries, and particularly the development of its cultural institutions. Cleveland in 1912 had a population of over a half million and was sixth in size in the nation. Its founder and first settlers had been New Englanders. Moses Cleaveland, surveyor for the Connecticut Land Company, reached the mouth of the Cuyahoga River on July 22, 1796 and laid out a town on its eastern bank. The site was within the Western Reserve, a tract of land owned by the Connecticut Land Company. Other New Englanders followed, and the struggling village held together despite the difficulties faced by all pioneers.

The War of 1812 increased trade in the area, but it was not until about 1830, after the Ohio Canal was built, that the village began to prosper. The railroad came in the mid-1800s, and when iron ore was discovered in the Mesabi Range on Lake Superior and oil was found in Titusville, Pennsylvania, the age of heavy industry began. With the building of the Ohio Canal, Irish and German workmen swelled the original population of transplanted New Englanders. With the development of industry, a large group of other foreigners was attracted here, and these later immigrants — many more Germans, plus Bohemians, Hungarians, Poles, Russians, Welsh, Italians, and others — found work in the factories.

Some of the descendants of the original New Englanders had amassed fortunes by 1912. They were upright men of character with a shrewd business sense; many had built large homes on Euclid Avenue, a thoroughfare known for its beauty. Streetcars travelled out Euclid Avenue, but in 1912, they turned off to run on Prospect Avenue between East 22nd and East 40th streets. Thus, the residents of Millionaires' Row, as this section of Euclid Avenue was sometimes called, would not be disturbed by the streetcars. Electric and gasoline automobiles passed these stately homes, but in those days there was very little traffic. Beginning in 1912, some of the leading families were moving farther east to the area around Wade Park, the Jeptha Wade Allotment, where magnificent residences soon lined East Boulevard, Magnolia, Hazel, and Mistletoe drives, as well as others.

These influential citizens led a busy social life, which included support for the arts. Those interested in music had to depend on small groups of musicians in their homes, musical clubs meeting in various places, or public concerts. The number of musical organizations in Cleveland during the second decade of this century is quite surprising. There were among others: the Tuesday Morning Musical Club, the Wednesday Musical Club, the Amateur Musical Club, the Harmonic Club, the Rubinstein Club, the Singers Club, and The Fortnightly Musical Club of Cleveland, the last two being still in existence. There were many concerts in these early years, and it can be said that almost all of the great musical artists of this period gave a concert in Cleveland. Many segments of the community shared an interest in music, but recent immigrants could not generally afford the public concerts or operas given in the city. Instead, music was a vital part of their lives in their homes and ethnic clubs.

While many Clevelanders were immersed in cultural and intellectual pursuits, there was at the same time a growing awareness of community and human needs. Prosperous citizens were becoming socially conscious and considered it a duty as well as a privilege to help those less fortunate. By 1912, then, there existed among these people not only an interest in culture, but also a desire to help the needy — attitudes which formed a fertile soil for the establishment of an organization with the purposes of The Cleveland Music School Settlement.

The creation of the School was due to a remarkable woman, Almeda C. Adams. She was born in Meadville, Pennsylvania, on February 26, 1865, and in her early years lived in Ohio, where her father was an itinerant clergyman. Having lost her sight when she was only six months old, she entered the state school for the blind in Columbus, Ohio, at the age of seven and remained there until she graduated at eighteen (or twenty, according to some sources).

An ambitious young lady, Miss Adams, through determination, perseverance, and hard work, usually accomplished what she set out to do. These traits were well demonstrated by the manner in which she succeeded in becoming a pupil at the New England Conservatory of Music. Though Almeda Adams was graduated in music from the Ohio School for the Blind, she found it impossible to secure a teaching position without further specialized training. Wishing to continue her musical education, she was immediately interested when friends told her of an offer by *The Ladies Home Journal.* The magazine would provide a scholarship at the New England Conservatory of Music for any girl who could secure a sizeable number of new subscribers; the length of instruction would be dependent upon the number of subscriptions obtained. Exactly when Almeda Adams started to work on this offer is not known, but in December 1891, a notice in the magazine stated that the offer could not continue much longer. In the January 1892 issue, the same notice was repeated, but it does not seem to have been printed after that. Probably, then, Miss Adams registered as a participant in the project by late 1891 or early 1892.

The magazine did not mention in its notice how many subscriptions were necessary to ensure a year's study at the Conservatory, but it must have been one thousand, as that was Miss Adams's goal. Most of her friends said that it was preposterous for her to attempt this; nevertheless, she was not deterred. Realizing that the tiny town where she lived with her family could never furnish enough orders, she decided to try larger towns, such as Tiffin. But since she had no money for the journey to Tiffin, she appealed to a woman of means in her father's congregation. Only after repeated requests did this woman agree to lend her the ten dollars necessary, and she gave it with the admonition that if Miss Adams did not repay the money, her father would lose his church. Needless to say, Almeda Adams repaid the loan out of her first earnings from rehearsing and conducting an operetta for a church benefit.

In Tiffin, Miss Adams supported herself by doing domestic work in the home of a minister, and while there she went from house to house soliciting subcriptions. Often she was met with kindness, but in some instances with cruel derision. She was told that she belonged at home, and that it was folly for a blind person to be engaged in such an undertaking. But she kept on. From Tiffin, Miss Adams went to Oberlin, then to Cincinnati. Finally, she arrived in Cleveland, where she was given assistance by Mrs. Oliver M. Brown; she had been matron of the Ohio School for the Blind and was, at this time, in charge of a boarding home on Walnut Avenue near East 9th Street. It was here that Almeda Adams went to live. The residents of this house lent a helping hand in securing subscriptions, and Jessie Glasier wrote an article in the *Cleveland Plain Dealer* telling about the aims and ambitions of Almeda Adams. The story was widely copied and subscriptions began rolling in. Since nothing succeeds like success, the friends of Miss Adams, hearing of this, decided to help. As a result, not a thousand, but two thousand five hundred subscriptions had been accumulated by the end of the year, enough to ensure two years at the New England Conservatory of Music in Boston.

Then came the sad blow. Upon learning that the winner was blind, the Conservatory informed Miss Adams that she could not be accepted. At this point, *The Ladies Home Journal* interceded and persuaded the Conservatory to give her a ten-week trial period; she proved herself to be more than qualified. In addition to studying voice, she completed theory under the noted Louis C. Elson and had exceptional opportunities to learn the teaching of public school music under Mr. George Veazie, one of the leading educators in this field. Attesting to the quality of her work, these teachers wrote:

June 23, 1894

Boston, Massachusetts

. . . I have never had a more conscientious and painstaking pupil, and the great intelligence she has displayed in the classroom makes me certain that she will be very successful as a teacher.

Louis C. Elson

New England Conservatory of Music

May 1, 1895

Chelsea, Massachusetts

It gives me great pleasure to recommend . . . Miss Almeda C. Adams, . . . of Lincoln Normal University, Lincoln, Nebraska.

Having been her instructor in that branch of school work, I can testify to her superior scholarship, her zeal and enthusiasm in her work, and I feel sure, that in what she undertakes, she will be eminently successful.

Respectfully,

G. A. Veazie

Instructor of Public School Music and

Superintendent of Music

When Miss Adams left the Conservatory in 1895, she had decided to accept a position to teach in the west, even though it meant leaving the Conservatory shortly before she had earned her degree. In Hoye's Directory of Lincoln, Nebraska, for 1896, the name of Almeda C. Adams appears; her occupation is given as teacher at Lincoln Normal University, her residence as Normal, a suburb of Lincoln. The Nebraska School for the Blind in Nebraska City issued a biennial report to the governor of the state, and the report for the years 1895-96 lists Almeda C. Adams as a teacher of voice and piano. Furthermore, it quotes at length the remarks of Miss Adams why a blind person is especially competent to teach voice. It seems, then, that the letter of recommendation from her teacher, Mr. Veazie, was written in support of her seeking application for a teaching position at the Nebraska School for the Blind. Miss Adams's obituary in the *Cleveland Plain Dealer* (September 10, 1949), stated that she taught piano and voice at the University of Nebraska, but this must be an error; perhaps it was a reference to Lincoln Normal University, since the State University of Nebraska has no record of Miss Adams's ever having taught there.

In a *Cleveland Plain Dealer* article, dated June 28, 1914, Rebecca French, who apparently interviewed Miss Adams, said that after teaching for five years in Nebraska, Miss Adams went to New York for further study in 1900. She remained there for a year, and because she possessed a fine voice and had had excellent training, she gave promise of a brilliant musical future. Her teacher said that if she came back for another year's study she would be ready to perform as a concert artist. Miss Adams had intended to do this, but her mother fell and broke her hip, an accident which crippled her for the rest of her life. Miss Adams felt constrained to help out at home and returned to Cleveland in 1901, as substantiated years later by her obituary. In Cleveland, she began directing a choral class at Central Friendly Inn and training singers at Alta House and Hiram House, experiences which introduced her to settlement houses.

The settlement movement was relatively new at this time. It had been started in 1884 in London, England, by Samuel Barnett, the vicar of St. Jude's Parish in Whitechapel. With the help of money raised mostly at Oxford University, Mr. Barnett had established a house of residence in Whitechapel for Oxford and Cambridge graduates. The theory was that residing in this poor district would enable the graduates to observe conditions at first hand. Their aim was to participate in the life of the neighborhood and to contribute to the well-being of its inhabitants. The graduates hoped to accomplish this by offering courses of study, and, more particularly, free programs of music and other entertainment as well as advice and counsel. This first settlement was named Toynbee Hall after Arnold Toynbee, the English social reformer and economist, whose interest in the needy and desire to be personally acquainted with them had led to his close association with the district of Whitechapel. This pioneer settlement made encouraging progress, and very shortly visitors from other countries came to study its operation. They brought the idea back to their home cities, the result being the establishment of institutions such as the Neighborhood Guild of the lower east side of New York in 1886 and Chicago's Hull House in 1889.

After Miss Adams returned to Cleveland, her father read a magazine article to her, and, to quote Miss Adams, "He read rather slowly, and it took over two hours. But the article told all about the wonderful work that David Mannes, a distinguished musician, was doing in a New York City settlement house devoted to music." When Mr. Adams put the magazine down, he said to his daughter, "You must do that thing for Cleveland. There is your work." Interestingly, an article about Mannes School, "The Value of Music School Settlements in Cities," by N. Curtis, appeared in *The Craftsman* for December 1911 (vol. XXI, no. 3). This article might well have been the one Miss Adams's father read to her, but we have no proof.

After hearing about the settlement in New York City, Almeda Adams began to dream about such an institution for Cleveland. Being a practical person, though, she did not rely upon written information alone and wanted to investigate for herself. She went to New York, visited the school, talked with its director, and was thoroughly impressed with the concept of a specialized settlement house for music. Upon her return home, she decided to present the idea to Adella Prentiss Hughes (Mrs. Felix S.). By this choice, Miss Adams demonstrated her good judgment, since Mrs. Hughes was an outstanding person in the cultural life of the city. Herself a pianist, she was also an impressario. With the phrase, "Adella Prentiss Hughes Presents," came a guarantee that musical events of the highest caliber were to appear in Cleveland — the Metropolitan Opera, the Diaghileff Ballet Russe, and orchestras conducted by

Arturo Toscanini, Gustav Mahler, Walter Damrosch, Leopold Stokowski, Frederick Stock, Karl Muck, Richard Strauss, and others.

Mrs. Hughes was also active in many organizations, including The Fortnightly Musical Club. With her great interest in music and desire to help in its promotion, Mrs. Hughes was sympathetic to the idea of such an institution as Almeda Adams envisioned for the city. Miss Adams is reported to have said:

> When I went out of her office, I was walking on air. Nothing mattered. She hadn't given any promises, she had simply said, "I wonder if that isn't something that The Fortnightly Club would be interested in. I will think about it."

She did think about it and then suggested the idea to the members of the Club, which included many prominent Clevelanders. A meeting, called by Mrs. John Huntington at her home to discuss the proposal, was presided over by Mayor Newton D. Baker, and Almeda Adams gave a talk. Minutes of The Fortnightly Musical Club of February 7, 1912, state:

> Moved by Mrs. Franklyn B. Sanders, seconded and carried, that Mesdames Arthur Bradley, L. Dean Holden, Felix S. Hughes, and Otis S. Southworth form a committee to assist with Miss Adams in organizing the Music School.

This committee worked most expeditiously, and by April 25, 1912, The Cleveland Music School Settlement was legally incorporated under the laws of Ohio. The articles of incorporation were witnessed and signed by the following incorporators: Miss Almeda Adams, Mrs. Arthur Bradley, Albert Rees Davis, Miss Grace B. Drake, Edward A. Foote, Mrs. Felix S. Hughes, Francis F. Prentiss, and Mrs. Andrew Squire. The purposes of the School, as stated in the articles of incorporation, were to make musical instruction possible for all by offering to both children and wage earners unable to pay studio fees the best instruction at a modest price; to provide scholarships for talented pupils who were not able to pay for lessons; to stimulate a love for music, and to become a factor in the musical life of the city.

Acting promptly, the incorporators met on April 29, 1912 at the Athletic Club Building. Mrs. Hughes acted as chairman and Miss Drake as secretary. The charter of the School was submitted to the incorporators, and the following persons were elected as members of the corporation's first board of trustees: Gardner Abbott, Miss Almeda Adams, E. M. Baker, Newton D. Baker, Mrs. Dudley S. Blossom, Mrs. Arthur Bradley, Albert Rees Davis, Miss Grace B. Drake, E. A. Foote, Mrs. L. Dean Holden, Mrs. Felix S. Hughes, Mrs. John Huntington, Mrs. R. Livingston Ireland, Mrs. Isaac Joseph, Frank B. Meade, Miss Mary Parsons, Arthur W. Pomeroy, Mrs. Charles W. Pratt, Francis F. Prentiss, Miss Julia Raymond, Miss Mary Raymond, Mrs. C. A. Ricks, Mrs. Ralph Silver, Mrs. Otis S. Southworth, Mrs. Andrew Squire, and Mrs. H. F. Stratton. This meeting of the incorporators adjourned and those of the newly elected trustees who were present convened the first meeting of the Settlement's board of trustees. Mrs. Hughes called upon Mr. Foote to present a code of rules and regulations for the School, and it was adopted. Next, a nominating committee was appointed to prepare a list of officers and committee chairmen for the next board meeting.

This meeting took place May 2, 1912, and the nominating committee presented the following slate:

President, Albert Rees Davis
Vice-Presidents, Francis F. Prentiss, Frank B.
      Meade, Mrs. Andrew Squire
Treasurer, Mrs. Charles W. Pratt
Secretary, Mrs. H. F. Stratton
Chairman of Finance Committee, E. A. Foote
Chairman of House Committee, Miss Grace B.
      Drake
Chairman of Membership Committee, Arthur W.
      Pomeroy
Chairman of Scholarship Committee, Mrs. Felix
      S. Hughes
Chairman of Music Committee, Mrs. Otis S.
      Southworth

The officers and committee chairmen were unanimously elected for a term of one year. They were well-known citizens of broad outlook and flexibility, witness to which was their readiness to make changes for the better — a characteristic that the trustees were to exhibit throughout the years. Already at this second board meeting, one of the bylaws of the corporation adopted at the previous meeting was considered and changed. This bylaw was an important one and provided for an executive committee to include the standing committee chairmen. All business, according to the bylaws, was to be "submitted to the committee which shall present it to the trustees in the form of a recommendation." The executive committee held its first meeting on May 6, 1912, and continued to meet twice a month; the regular board meetings were held once a month initially, but only twice or three times a year later.

In the beginning years, the executive committee was referred to as the executive board. Mr. E. A. Foote was elected its first chairman; he had already taken a leadership role in drawing up the bylaws and regulations, which included provisions for financing. The bylaws established a membership plan in which a gift of one thousand dollars or more made the donor a founder; a gift of five hundred to one thousand dollars a patron; and so forth down to five dollars for an associate membership. Contributors were called subscribers and were referred to as such in most reports. This membership and the students' fees, plus the benefit concerts and Christmas caroling program, to be described later, were to constitute the financing of the School in its early period.

The original committee from The Fortnightly Musical Club which had been appointed to assist Miss Adams in organizing the School recommended that the Club become a subscriber. It contributed one thousand dollars and became the first founder member of the Settlement. In the files of The Fortnightly Musical Club, there is a handwritten note on Settlement letterhead, dated September 26, 1912, which reads:

Mrs. Robert Crowell:

The executive board of The Cleveland Music School Settlement begs to acknowledge most gratefully the generous gift of The Fortnightly Musical Club, and takes great pleasure in inscribing its name as the first founder.

Very truly,
Marion Prentiss Stratton
Secretary

Individuals who became founders shortly thereafter were: Mrs. Dudley S. Blossom, Francis E. Drury, Mrs. Francis E. Drury, Mrs. James E. Ferris, Samuel Mather, Mrs. M. B. Otis, and Mrs. Lyman H. Treadway.

Now that the Settlement was organized, the next important step was to find a suitable location and someone to direct the School's activities. After a thorough canvass of available properties, space which included three rooms in Goodrich House (at the corner of St. Clair Avenue and East 6th Street) was selected, and Miss Linda W. Sampson from the east was engaged as superintendent. The reader will notice that Miss Sampson, during the years of her service, is referred to as superintendent, head, head resident, or director of the School; these titles all appear in the minutes and various reports. It is interesting that the first executive of the school was a trained nurse. She had been known to Miss Grace B. Drake, one of the original trustees, having nursed Miss Drake's brother; perhaps it was through this connection that Miss Sampson was brought to the attention of the board. Though she was not a musician, she proved to be a very wise choice for the Settlement. Those who knew her said that she was the most motherly, loving woman, who expected the best from everyone and always got it.

At a meeting of the board of trustees in July 1912, seventeen memberships, or subscriptions, were reported. Also, it was noted that Miss Almeda Adams had been chosen as head of the voice department, and Walter Logan, a well-known Cleveland musician, as head of the violin department. It was moved to engage Mrs. Gertrude Kemmerling as the first teacher in the piano department, and the secretary was instructed to invite the new faculty to meet with the trustees at the Settlement. Further, the trustees accepted the executive committee's recommendation to invite Miss Crawford of the New York Music School Settlement to come to Cleveland for the opening of the School and to remain for one month to assist with the launching of this unique settlement for the city.

October 1, 1912 was chosen for the formal inauguration, and Miss Grace B. Drake was asked to take charge of publicity for the big event. When the trustees met at Goodrich House for this occasion, the rooms had been furnished and a piano had been purchased. The School started propitiously with fifty applicants, and by the end of the first month, there were one hundred and thirty, of which one hundred and eleven were found eligible. And so, the dream had become reality.

At this point, it is interesting to note the founding dates of other major cultural and educational institutions which followed the organization of The Cleveland Music School Settlement in 1912. They are as follows: 1915, The Cleveland Play House; 1916, The Cleveland Museum of Art; 1918, The Cleveland Orchestra; 1920 The Cleveland Institute of Music and the Cleveland Museum of

Natural History. This record stands as a tribute to the dedication and generosity of the prominent Clevelanders of that era; many of these citizens, both men and women, were involved in the establishment of more than one institution. Special mention should be made of Adella Prentiss Hughes, who took a leading role in helping Almeda Adams organize the Settlement, and who later was recognized as the "Mother of the Cleveland Orchestra."

On January 27, 1913, the first annual meeting of the Settlement's board of trustees was held at Goodrich House. The secretary, Marion Prentiss Stratton, gave a resume of the School's founding, and reports of the superintendent, Linda W. Sampson, and the treasurer were read. Mr. Foote, chairman of the executive committee, gave an analysis of the cost of operating the School, the net amount being placed at one dollar and fifty-four cents per hour. The names of the one-year and two-year term trustees were read, and the following three-year trustees were nominated and elected: Mrs. Henry Chisholm, E. A. Foote, Miss Josephine Grasselli, Grover Higgins, Fred Joseph, John MacGregor, Frank Muhlhauser, Mrs. D. Z. Norton, Miss Mary Raymond, and Mrs. George N. Sherwin.

At the board meeting in February, Mr. E. A. Foote was elected as president, and Mrs. Andrew Squire was re-elected as vice-president. Two other vice-presidents were chosen, Mr. Fred Joseph and Mrs. D. Z. Norton, while Mrs. Charles W. Pratt and Mrs. H. F. Stratton were to continue as treasurer and secretary, respectively. It was agreed that the bylaws needed revision again, and Mr. Foote assumed this task with the assistance of Mr. Joseph.

The generosity of Grace B. Drake enabled Superintendent Sampson to be sent as a delegate to a conference of the National Association of Music School Societies held in Boston in April 1913. A written history of the Settlement was submitted to the Association and was incorporated in its year book. Miss Sampson reported to the delegates that the enrollment of The Cleveland Music School Settlement was two hundred and seven. During the first six months of operation, seven hundred and eighty lessons had been given in piano, violin, cello, cornet, and voice; class instruction was offered in sight reading, harmony, and musical history. Upon her return to Cleveland, she was pleased to tell the board that the delegates were impressed with the remarkable progress of the Settlement. It became a member of the National Association of Music School Societies a few months later.

In all non-profit organizations, particularly those without endowments, a considerable amount of time must be spent by the trustees in securing financial assistance. The Settlement was no exception to this rule, and as it grew and the aspirations of the trustees and faculty mounted, the need for additional monies was recognized. Several projects were undertaken, and on October 18, 1913 notice was given in *Town Topics,* the magazine devoted to social functions in Cleveland, that a concert under the direction of Miss Almeda Adams would be presented for the benefit of the Settlement at the Euclid Avenue Baptist Church. Pupils of Miss Adams would be assisted by Miss Nella Springer, a talented young violinist. No tickets were to be sold, but a silver offering was to be taken. Other fund-raising was suggested by Miss Adams — the formation of a Pipers Club composed of children who, through their parents' interest in the School, wanted to help their less fortunate peers. This was a successful idea first introduced by the New York Music School Settlement. Parents of means thought that this was a lovely way to teach their children to help others. A child might become a member of the Pipers Club upon a contribution of all or part of a scholarship. In return, the young scholarship recipients were to give two concerts annually for the Pipers Club members. Miss Harriet S. Eells, a trustee, accepted the chairmanship of the Club. Another project was the printing and distribution of a pamphlet prepared by A. C. Rogers, which would promote the work of the Settlement. The trustees were public relations-minded even in those years, and the pamphlet was sent not only to all the subscribers to encourage them to renew their donations, but to others as well in order to gain new friends.

Early in the year, Miss Sampson had told of the poverty of some of the families who struggled to pay twenty-five cents a lesson. She proposed that fifty cents a lesson be paid by those who were able to do so. The executive committee disapproved of this sliding scale of fees and turned down the suggestion. However, this committee did decide several months later to charge those who were eighteen years of age or over, and working, fifty cents a lesson.

By the end of the Settlement's first year of operation in 1913, there were already significant trends in its development. Eighteen nationalities were represented in the enrollment, which demonstrated the catholicity of the School; also, one of the trustees, Mrs. Andrew Squire, had suggested that a black woman should be chosen who would help to interest the black community in the School. The Settlement could always point with pride to its early and genuine concern for all residents of Cleveland. During the initial year, too, Dr. Richard Dexter had volunteered medical assistance to the pupils. Such offers of help were to be reported countless times throughout the School's history. For the holiday season, the trustees evidenced their thoughtfulness by giving a Christmas party for the students, a tradition still carried on.

Because of the growth in enrollment and the expanded curriculum, there was a need for a dean to coordinate the various functions of the School. The board appointed Walter Logan, head of the violin department, to the position; he was a versatile musician, being also a conductor and composer. Upon graduation from Oberlin College, Mr. Logan continued his studies in Chicago and later joined the faculty at Northwestern University. A member of the Chicago Symphony Orchestra for several seasons, he returned to Cleveland in 1912 for his post at the Settlement and to conduct choral, orchestra, and band groups. Mr. Logan was to become a member of The Cleveland Orchestra under Nikolai Sokoloff when it was founded in 1918 by Adella Prentiss Hughes.

As 1914 dawned, the trustees were confronted with financial problems, but at their meeting in February, they were given good news. Madame Emma Eames, a singer of international reputation, who had family connections in Cleveland and who had recently retired from her musical career, had offered to contribute her services for a recital as a benefit for the Settlement. This magnanimous gesture was received with enthusiasm, and the recital, held in the Statler Hotel Ballroom, was a social and musical triumph, *Town Topics* (March 21, 1914) had this to say of the evening:

> Except for some of the gala evenings at the opera, Cleveland has perhaps never known a more brilliant musical event than the concert for the benefit of the Music School Settlement given in the Statler ballroom a week ago. . . . Fifteen hundred dollars will be added to the treasury of the Settlement to be used in what ex-President Eliot of Harvard well characterizes as an admirable opportunity to invest private money in the happiness and contentment of children, and Emma Eames is henceforth enrolled as the first honorary member of its board of

trustees.
This occasion had been made possible through the efforts of Mrs.
Adella Prentiss Hughes, who had persuaded Madame Eames to
donate her services. Not only had Mrs. Hughes acted as manager
of the concert and secured the use of the Statler Ballroom at no cost,
but she also was the accompanist for Madame Eames. A small item
in the minutes of the executive committee in March 1914 is of interest:

> Announcement was made that Mr. John D.
> Rockefeller had sent twenty-five dollars for the
> purchase of tickets for the Eames Recital, for the
> poor pupils.

In April 1914, the School was honored by the visit of David
Mannes, head of the New York Music School Settlement, and his
wife, both of whom Almeda Adams had met in New York. From
all accounts, this was an exciting and meaningful time for those
involved with the Settlement. The trustees gave a reception for Mr.
and Mrs. Mannes at the home of Mr. and Mrs. Francis E. Drury,
then located on Euclid Avenue at East 86th Street. Entertainment
for the guests was provided by a quartet from the Settlement and
James H. Rogers, who played the Drurys' Aeolian organ. A
composer and organist of note, he was also music critic of the
Cleveland News, and later of the *Cleveland Plain Dealer.* Mr.
Mannes then gave a talk on the ideals of a music school settlement.
Among the things he said were the following:

> When a physician takes up his residence in a city
> he says, "In what hospital can I give my services?"
> Every serious-minded musician in Cleveland should
> look upon the Music School Settlement here as the
> local music hospital. He ought to offer some of his
> services. There is no better place to prepare the
> musical soil in Cleveland, with its large foreign
> population. . . . Musically, the Settlement work
> ought to be the greatest thing here. . . . Service like
> Dean Logan's to the community cannot be
> overestimated. . . . The financial and moral support
> he has received from broad-minded citizens is an
> investment that in time will pay great dividends . . .

Other events of the year demonstrated a particular trustee's largesse
and willingness to help the School. Through the generosity of Mrs.
R. Livingston Ireland, Walter Logan went to visit the New York

Music School Settlement in order to learn more about the work being done there; Mrs. Ireland also made it possible for Almeda Adams to visit Hull House in Chicago to bring back new ideas.

The School continued to expand in many directions, especially in ensemble work, and more space was needed. The whole upper floor of Goodrich House, comprising eleven rooms, was acquired, but the rent was less by virtue of the fact that some of the staff resided there. At this time the faculty consisted of ten salaried and nine volunteer teachers. New were an orchestra of twenty-six members, a children's chorus of thirty, and a dancing class. This was a great deal of activity for a fledgling organization but, nevertheless, personal attention was given to particular cases of sorrow or need. The pupils felt that Miss Sampson, "the lady at the Settlement," was a sympathetic friend.

The revision of the bylaws and regulations had been completed by President Foote and Fred Joseph and had been accepted by the trustees at their October meeting in 1914. Another important action was taken at this meeting — recognition was given to Almeda Adams by conferring on her the honorary title of Founder in token of her devoted efforts which had served as a catalyst for the creation of the School.

In November the well-known concert pianist, Ralph Leopold, who had been visiting his sister, Mrs. Newton D. Baker, was prevented from returning to Berlin by the outbreak of World War I. He was also a great authority on Richard Wagner, and *Town Topics* (November 14, 1914) recorded the following:

> A fine feature of this season is the promised series
> of Wagner lectures to be given at The Cleveland
> Music School Settlement on alternate Monday
> evenings, beginning November 23rd, by Ralph
> Leopold, of Berlin . . .

Before coming to the Settlement, Mr. Logan had founded and was conducting an amateur orchestra, known as the Young People's Symphony Orchestra. It was composed of wage-earning young men and women who rehearsed once a week, and the practice sessions were now being conducted at the School. In December of 1914, Mr. Logan asked the trustees to allow the Orchestra to be affiliated with the Settlement, but with the proviso that the trustees would not be liable for any of its financial obligations. After careful consideration, the trustees agreed that the School would take this musical entity under its aegis with the understanding that one concert would be given a year, and that the trustees would not be called upon to solicit funds for its maintenance. They expected that the Orchestra would be self-sufficient, charging admission or collecting fees for performances elsewhere as it had been doing.

To return to the financial condition of the School — in spite of the success of the Eames concert — there was still a need for additional funds toward the end of the year. Mrs. George N. Sherwin, chairman of the faculty committee, announced at a board meeting in October 1914 that:

> The present financial condition is such that we will not be able to raise sufficient funds to carry on our work. It seems wise, therefore, to cut the number of hours of our paid teachers to six hours per week and fill their places with volunteer teachers, thus maintaining our efficiency and usefulness at less cost.

The volunteer teachers at the time in the piano department were Mrs. B. P. Bourland, Miss Frances Hartline, Mrs. Walter G. Stern, Miss Walpole, and Miss Jean Webster; in the violin department, Miss Frances Birous and Mrs. Caroline Harter Williams, and, in the voice department, Mrs. Newton D. Baker and Mrs. Sterling Newell.

Lest anyone think that the quality of instruction was reduced by using these dedicated volunteer teachers, several of whom were trustees, it is only necessary to give the background of two or three at random. Mrs. Caroline Harter Williams was a graduate of the Geneva Conservatory of Music in Switzerland and for three years had been a member of the faculty of Oberlin Conservatory; Miss Jean Webster had recently returned from years of study in Berlin and Paris, and Mrs. Sterling Newell had had three years of study in Paris.

An unusual money-raising plan was proposed by Trustee Grace B. Drake. This was the Christmas caroling program, which Miss Drake was permitted to start, and which was to endure year after year. Groups of children all over the city and suburbs were recruited and trained by the School, and on Christmas Eve they went out and sang carols in front of every home that had a lighted candle in the window; donations were solicited from these homes after the singing. This undertaking entailed a tremendous amount of organization and was dependent upon countless volunteers to transport the children, to stay with them, and to supervise their caroling as they moved from house to house. It also required considerable publicity to alert the various suburbs and communities, so that they could organize their groups and induce the residents to place candles in their windows. Happily, the enterprise proved to be well worth the efforts expended. The very first year, the carolers took in more than thirteen hundred dollars on December 24, 1914. It was a remarkable undertaking when one considers that the singers and those who transported them were away from their families on Christmas Eve.

The School's financial condition was still critical and in order to interest new people in the School, Almeda Adams received permission to talk to church organizations, especially their young people's societies. Superintendent Sampson also wanted to help; she offered to relinquish the increase of salary which the board had voted to give her until such time as the School's finances were improved. With such devotion, the School was able to continue operating.

At the meeting of the board of trustees in January 1915, Mrs. George N. Sherwin was elected president. As chairman of the faculty committee, she had given invaluable service to the School; as a member of The Fortnightly Musical Club, her election provided an important link to this Club that had been so generous to the Settlement. An innovation under Mrs. Sherwin's presidency was the addition of a social service committee to the regular standing committees, the need for which had been pointed out to the board by Almeda Adams. The committee had expanded the social service work of the School and had also taken over the administration of an emergency loan fund.

In March, the Young People's Symphony Orchestra, assisted by Mrs. Winifred Lawrence Ingersoll, gave a concert in Engineers' Hall. Later in the year, this orchestra and that of Pilgrim Church merged, an affiliation which brought many new players under the direction of Walter Logan and made it possible for the orchestra to give two more public concerts annually. The new official name was "The Young People's Symphony Orchestra of The Music School Settlement."

In April, David Mannes, who had retired as director of the New York Music School Settlement, paid a return visit to Cleveland. This time, Miss Josephine Grasselli, a trustee, arranged a tea at the School, to which all board members were invited as well as faculty and a few guests selected by the president, about sixty-five in all. Of some interest today is the fact that the food for the tea (bread, fillings for sandwiches, mayonnaise, cakes, and nuts) cost five dollars according to Miss Grasselli's report.

In June, the closing concert of the year was given by the pupils of the School, and it was as one account reported, "a source of much gratification to the teachers and of satisfaction to the promoters of this musical beneficence." In October, Miss Sampson reported to the trustees that the settlements of Cleveland had federated and were holding monthly meetings. The Cleveland Music School Settlement joined the group and paid two dollars a year dues.

This year, 1915, the finances of the Settlement had become more stable. The Christmas caroling helped by bringing in fifteen hundred dollars, and from other sources the earnings of the year (annual subscribers, tuition fees, the interest from the monies provided by The Fortnightly Musical Club and the benefit concert of Emma Eames) amounted to more than seven thousand dollars. Thus, the annual meeting held in January 1916 had a good report. A fillip at the end of this meeting was the performance by students, a boy violinist being of particular interest because of his background. A Hungarian gypsy, he had been rescued from performing in a saloon two years previously by a visiting nurse; the boy had been taught by a "fake" teacher and was playing "On the Mississippi." His widowed mother, who took in washing for a living, paid this teacher seven dollars a month, a large sum in those days, for her son's lessons. Fortunately, the boy was now receiving proper instruction at the Settlement and was making good progress.

Early in 1916, the trustees learned of a situation — embarrassing to them — in the housekeeping expenses of the resident staff, now numbering nine. It seems that Miss Sampson and Miss Drake had personally paid for the furnishing; in addition, the money paid by resident boarders was not sufficient to meet the expenses, so Miss Sampson and Miss Drake had themselves been paying the deficit each month. The trustees felt that such a situation was beneath the dignity of the School; as a result, an inventory of the furnishings was made, and the two women were paid a fair sum for what they had purchased. In addition, a housekeeper was engaged to relieve Miss Sampson and Miss Drake of any responsibility for the Settlement household.

As each year passed, there were usually special occasions which brought the School to the attention of the public. One of these was the operetta, *Snow White,* presented by the chorus classes in April

1916 at Knickerbocker Theatre (8315 Euclid Avenue) as a part of The Fortnightly Musical Club's series of young people's concerts. Almeda Adams, in her report of the event to the board, paid high tribute to Miss Drake's training of the children. Many requests for a repeat performance had been received.

Another outstanding event occurred also in April, when the Young People's Symphony Orchestra gave its spring concert in Engineers' Hall. What made this concert very special was the fact that, in honor of the tercentenary of William Shakespeare's death, tableaux, Morris dances, and Elizabethan music were a part of the program. Taking part in the tableaux were members of the Amateur Musical Club, many of whom were Settlement trustees. The tableaux were presented in a portmanteau theatre, and they were posed under the direction of Frederick C. Gottwald of The Cleveland School of Art (later The Cleveland Institute of Art), who spent countless hours arranging them. *Town Topics,* that inestimable recorder of the Cleveland scene, gives the salient features in its issue of April 29, 1916:

> A Spring concert of the Orchestra of the Settlement under the direction of Walter Logan took place, as is the usual custom, at Engineers' Hall. . . . The audience on these occasions assumes a fashionable aspect through the presence of the supporters of the Settlement, who gather with their friends, and friends of the performers, to applaud the results of the season's study, and to show appreciation for the genial and untiring efforts of Mr. Walter Logan, to whose intelligent instruction and enthusiastic guiding the faculty of the Settlement owes much of its success . . . there was to be a combination on this occasion of a Shakespeare celebration with the orchestral program . . . Elizabethan Morris dances, somewhat resembling the figures of a Virginia reel, done by six young men and women, friends of the Settlement, in pale and dark blue smocks, made an interlude between the orchestral part of the program and the twelve tableaux from Shakespeare's plays. . . . The poses, costuming, and stage arrangement with portable scenic accessories, all showed careful study and patient, devoted and long continued effort on the part of the stage committee. . . .

Trustee Arthur Pomeroy and the corps of able
assistants from the art school deserve unstinted
praise for the smooth and effective presentation of
difficult subjects. Recitations, admirably given by
Mr. William Haworth, preceded each picture, with
apt quotations from the play chosen.

The Young People's Symphony Orchestra was not the only
orchestra connected with the Settlement — there were two others,
the Senior and the Junior Orchestras. In 1916, the latter had been
before the public with much success on several occasions. For
example, it had appeared at the Educational Alliance, the Woodland
Avenue Library, the home of Mrs. K. F. Gill for an East End
Neighborhood House benefit, and at the United States district court
for the entertainment of newly naturalized citizens.

The trustees approved a plan to hold the annual meeting in October
instead of January, to coincide with the school year, and, in another
prudent move, appointed a budget committee. They granted
permission for the School to join the National Federation of
Settlements, and in an effort to enhance the standards of teaching,
two department heads were named: Nathan Fryer for the piano
department and Mrs. Harvey D. Goulder for the voice department.
In addition, the trustees invited the three department heads, Mr.
Logan, Mr. Fryer, and Mrs. Goulder, to attend executive committee
meetings.

That the School had the respect of the city government was proved
by several decisions made by Cleveland's director of public service.
The Young People's Symphony Orchestra was now permitted to use
the library of music owned by the city of Cleveland and to retain
music and books longer than two weeks; also, the Orchestra was
given exclusive use of various drums that formerly belonged to the
municipal orchestra. The Cleveland board of education recognized
the Settlement by offering to assume the expense of lessons for several
sightless children. Not only were the achievements of the School
acknowledged locally, but nearly all the articles in the spring quarterly
of the *National Music School Review* described its work.

At the annual meeting held in October 1916, Mrs. Otis S.
Southworth was elected to the presidency. At this time, plans were
already being formulated for the Christmas caroling, since more
interest than ever seemed to be manifested in this project. Groups
of singers from Shaker Heights and Collinwood to Rocky River

offered their services, and on the west side alone, thirty-two groups of singers were formed. Churches, their Sunday schools, and other organizations volunteered. The 1916 carolers sang on Public Square to open the community Christmas of the city, and then they moved to the juvenile court for more singing. On Christmas Eve, carolers sang on the steps of all the churches on Euclid Avenue and throughout the residential areas. This project had grown beyond all expectation, and singing Christmas carols for the Settlement had become a significant community activity.

In January 1917 the Young People's Symphony Orchestra played at the Hippodrome Theatre downtown, an appearance for which it was paid two hundred dollars, and it was planning to give five Sunday afternoon concerts at popular prices in Grays' Armory. Though this orchestra was completely under the auspices of the Settlement, its personnel still did not consist solely of faculty and students at the School. In fact, it was planned at one time during the year to place notices about the Orchestra in libraries and other appropriate places to attract amateur musicians. In some instances, musicians who played "unusual" instruments had to be hired for certain concerts. "Unusual" was a term used by the School to designate instruments not always included in orchestral works and not taught at the Settlement. The Musical Arts Association, formed for the purpose of furthering the interests of music in the community, and which in 1918 created The Cleveland Orchestra, had been generously providing funds to the School for such instrumentalists.

The Young People's Orchestra gave its regular spring concert in April at the Duchess Theatre on Euclid Avenue near East 55th Street. This was a joint program with the Neighborhood Players of New York City, which presented a one-act play by Lord Dunsany. The uniting of these two groups evidenced the excellent reputation of The Cleveland Music School Settlement in New York City. Though the performance was not a financial success, the trustees felt that the program had "contributed towards the artistic development of the city." They decided that the next series of concerts should not be advertised under the name of the Settlement, and efforts were to be made to make the public realize that this series was being presented for the whole community. Unfortunately, the next concert in November also failed financially, and the trustees came to the conclusion that the Young People's Symphony Orchestra could not be self-sustaining. Consequently, its funds were to be treated as a separate entity and its operation handled exclusively by the orchestra committee of the Settlement.

The School had to watch its income and expenses closely — contributions were coming in slowly and forty-four people had neglected to renew their membership subscriptions. Trustees were urged to approach some of the people personally. It was most fortunate that The Musical Arts Association continued to support the Young People's Symphony Orchestra and had also agreed to give fifty dollars per month for one year to Miss Muriel Abbott. This would enable her to teach violin and ensemble music ten hours per week. Despite such assistance, the budget committee was authorized in April to consider reducing expenses for the coming year.

In connection with finances, it is interesting to note that at one meeting of the executive committee, Superintendent Sampson produced the following rather astonishing figures: rental for the Settlement per month, one hundred and twenty-six dollars; income from rooms rented to outsiders, one hundred and fifteen dollars per month; actual cost of rent per month, eleven dollars. Another surprising item: Miss Drake conducted a dancing class on Thursday evenings attended by more than one hundred people; cost of attendance for each person, five cents.

At the end of May in 1917, the National Conference on Community Music was held in New York City. The president of the Settlement, Mrs. Otis S. Southworth, and Dean Logan attended, the latter being the official delegate from the School. In June, the National Federation of Settlements held its regular convention in Valencia, Pennsylvania, and Superintendent Sampson went to that meeting.

The entrance of the United States into World War I in the spring had little effect on the Settlement at first. The trustees endorsed Mr. E. A. Foote's suggestion that at all concerts given by the Young People's Symphony Orchestra "The Star Spangled Banner" should be played. By the summer, though, the war was making an impact, and people were planting war gardens. Seeds had in fact been given to the pupils of the School for this purpose. An interesting sidelight in this connection turned up in *Town Topics* (August 25, 1917):

> The velvet smooth front lawn before the residence
> of Mr. and Mrs. E. S. Burke, Jr., at Magnolia and
> Mistletoe drives is no more. In its place, a fine war
> garden is nearing harvest perfection. . . . That the

> harvest crop will be a fine one, everyone in the
> Rosedale school district knows. The Burke garden
> is one of special pride to the committee from that
> district . . . . Not many gardens can boast, however,
> of having had beautiful front lawns torn up for
> them.

That this war garden was mentioned in society news is witness to the prominence of its owners and the imposing nature of the residence. That it would eventually become the main home of The Cleveland Music School Settlement was not yet known.

At the annual meeting in October, Mrs. Southworth was re-elected as president for the next year. From then until the end of the year, the Christmas caroling program was the chief concern of the School. Miss Grace B. Drake had resigned as chairman of this event, and Mrs. Ward Fenton, Jr., and Mrs. Harvey D. Goulder assumed her responsibilities. "Never in the history of the world," said Mrs. Fenton, "has there been a time when so many hearts have longed for peace." (*Town Topics,* October 27, 1917). The success in previous years, as well as innumerable requests to continue the custom, had influenced the board to repeat the program in a war year. Though the weather was inclement, the caroling was a success again. The Singers Club had had a group of carolers at the Opera House and the Hippodrome, and Almeda Adams, E. A. Foote, and Felix S. Hughes took a group of young singers to several movie houses. The total sum collected was three thousand nine hundred and forty-eight dollars and ninety-seven cents.

Though World War I was still in progress, the Settlement was able to continue many of its normal activities in 1918. However, there were several great changes for the School. The first was the resignation of Superintendent Sampson, which took place in April, and the departure at the same time of Miss Grace B. Drake, who, as a trustee, had started the Christmas caroling. The two women, known for their great dignity and dedication, had decided to embark upon a new life. They went to New York City to become associated with the Allerton House for Women, Miss Drake as manager and Miss Sampson as head housekeeper. Miss Sampson had been a dedicated and tireless leader for the Settlement, and the trustees recognized her efficiency and fine record with the gift of a necklace and a letter of appreciation; she was also granted her salary for the entire month of April. Dean Logan was sent to Boston to interview Mrs. Catherine

Saunders of the Boston Music School Settlement, and she later came
to the School to meet with the trustees. They were favorably
impressed, and Mrs. Saunders was named director.

During the year, there were certain repercussions from the war
that affected the School. The Children's Chorus, directed by Almeda
Adams, was asked to sing on the Public Square in May for the
beginning of the war chest drive. The board gave its permission for
this service, and the chorus sang at various other gatherings during
the drive. Later in September, the trustees discussed the advisability
of establishing a school for band players with specific training for
positions in military service. The program was to be coordinated with
the war department, but plans were cancelled when a letter arrived
from Newton D. Baker, one of the original trustees of the Settlement, who had been appointed secretary of war in 1916. He expressed
appreciation for the offer, but said that since the armistice in
November and demobilization, the Army music school on
Governor's Island could supply all the necessary personnel for army
bands.

During the war days of 1918, concerts by the Young People's
Symphony Orchestra were among the activities particularly
appreciated by the community. This orchestra, however, was to
become a problem in a short time. Despite the deficit of eleven
hundred dollars incurred by the five concerts given in 1917 at popular
prices (ten cents for general admission, fifteen and twenty-five cents
for reserved seats), the Orchestra planned two Sunday afternoon
concerts that included community singing under the direction of
Harper Garcia Smythe at Grays' Armory in January. In May, the
Orchestra participated in the regular spring concert under the
direction of Walter Logan. There were now three orchestras at the
Settlement besides the Young People's — the senior, junior,
elementary — and they also performed at this concert under the
direction, respectively, of Mr. Logan, Vaugh D. Cahill, and Hal G.
Van Aikin. It must have been a very long program, as there were
also pieces for piano and violin, a string quartet, and excerpts from
the operetta, *A Modern Cinderella,* composed by Almeda Adams
and performed by her pupils. One review (*Town Topics,* June 1,
1918) said that the trustees and faculty of the Settlement were to
be congratulated upon the interesting display of their season's efforts.
That was an apt comment for a concert with performances by four
different orchestras.

In 1918, the School's services had become so well known that various organizations asked the Settlement for assistance. Among these were the Euclid Avenue Baptist Church, seeking a director for its Sunday school orchestra, and the Negro Welfare Association, wanting a leader for a chorus of sixty people. The Settlement endeavored to fulfill these requests to the best of its ability and entered into mutually helpful associations with other nearby organizations. The Cleveland Museum of Art had loaned prints and other material for exhibition in the School's office, and its director, Frederic Allen Whiting, had offered the service to the Settlement of the Museum's curator of music, Thomas Whitney Surette.

In June, Almeda Adams was granted a year's leave of absence for study in New York at the Mannes School. Not only did the Settlement have excellent and well-known teachers, but it allowed them time for further study, a policy pursued to this day. While Miss Adams was in New York, one of her former pupils taught some of her voice students. The more advanced ones were instructed by Lila Robeson, a prominent Cleveland singer, who had performed with the Metropolitan Opera and who was at that time teaching on a limited basis at the Settlement.

A major event of the year was the moving of the School to a new location. Several years earlier there had been rumors that Goodrich House was for sale. An option to buy had indeed been taken on the facility, and the trustees began looking for new housing. However, the option was not exercised, so the matter was dropped. But in 1918, the trustees thought it would be desirable for the School to locate in a building with more space, one that would be more accessible for most of its students. By August, the Settlement was offered the lease of such a property at 7033 Euclid Avenue, the former Henry W. Corning residence. Besides the larger quarters in the home itself, there was a barn which could be, and subsequently was, remodeled to provide a rehearsal hall for the four orchestras of the Settlement, the chorus, and the dancing class; there was also enough space for rental to other organizations. The School moved into its new home in late October or early November; the exact date is not recorded. *Town Topics* (November 30, 1918) carried the following notice:

> Through the generous offer of a friend to assume
> the rent of a house suitable for the growing activities
> of the music school, the dream of the board of
> trustees, that it might be possible to move the

School to a location easy of access for its four
hundred pupils, has come true.

No word of such a benefactor appears in the minutes of the board,
undoubtedly to preserve the desired anonymity. It is certain,
however, that the expenses of alterations and the moving itself were
assumed by the trustees. The alterations had to be postponed because
of the "flu epidemic," that devastating disaster for the community
and the country. The School, like all others in the city, had to be
closed from October 8th to November 13th.

In December, the regular Christmas caroling program was again
undertaken, despite the gloom cast by the epidemic. The
administration felt that it would be especially appropriate this year
to celebrate the end of World War I. Suggestions for procedure
noted:

If your group has been prevented from rehearsing
due to any influenza cases, it is suggested that you
call an open air rehearsal fifteen minutes before
starting on Tuesday. Practice the first verse of each
carol which everyone knows, and thus carry out the
singing on Christmas Eve as planned.

The financial report of the carols recorded, "Probably $3,500 will
approximate the net results by the time the bills come in."

In 1919 the executive committee and the board held many discussions on the future of the Young People's Symphony Orchestra, its
part in the work of the School, and its funding. As had been noted,
this orchestra was having difficulties. Besides being unsuccessful
financially, it was refused the use of union musicians to fill in for
players of "unusual" instruments. Too, the Orchestra was banned
from giving concerts in many places, because it encroached upon
professional players. Furthermore, the newly formed Cleveland
Orchestra was available. The trustees studied these problems in
depth, and many questions were asked — was the Young People's
Symphony Orchestra an actual or only a nominal part of the Settlement, since most of its players were not students at the School? If
not a part of the Settlement, should it be abandoned? If a part of
the Settlement, should it be a separate department? What was its
real purpose? Originally, an amateur orchestra organized to play for
pleasure, should it now be considered as an educational facility to
give training for future earning capacity? If this were to be its
function, how could the School manage players of "unusual"

instruments? Should the amateur players be regarded as pupils of the School, even though they only played in the Orchestra? Above all, how could the Settlement finance the concerts, each of which cost between three and four hundred dollars?

After careful consideration, the board took over the Young People's Symphony Orchestra; it also determined that the Orchestra's primary purpose in the future should be to develop orchestral playing ability among the pupils.

The trustees also approved a sum of money to buy "unusual" instruments, hoping to encourage the students to play them and to make unnecessary the hiring of union musicians. In this connection, the Francis E. Drurys offered their home for a series of four concerts to be given by members of the faculty and advanced students, in which the "unusual" musical instruments would be featured. The board also accepted the fifteen hundred dollars which Mrs. Adella Prentiss Hughes had urged The Musical Arts Association to give the Settlement for the financing of the concerts by the Young People's Symphony Orchestra in 1919-1920. This gift had been approved by the trustees, only after they had been assured that the School would be completely free to determine the Orchestra's policies. In the early part of 1919, before all these matters had been settled, three trustees generously came to the rescue and financed three concerts by the Orchestra: one at The Cleveland Museum of Art, paid for by Mrs. Drury; another at Trinity Cathedral, underwritten by Mrs. Andrew Squire, and the usual spring concert, the cost of which was taken care of by Frank Muhlhauser.

This year, 1919, the trustees contemplated reprinting the bylaws and regulations of the School. However, when a copy of these, as amended by E. A. Foote and Fred Joseph in 1914, had been perused, the trustees changed their minds. The budget in 1914 had been four thousand dollars. Obviously, there had been some great changes in operation, administration, activities, and location, and the board decided it would be more sensible to bring the bylaws and regulations up to date before having them printed again. A committee was then appointed to make the revisions, and a new governing document was presented at the annual meeting of the board in October. It was accepted, and among the changes was the date of the annual meeting, which was moved to the end rather than the beginning of the school year. Time has proved this to be a good decision, and the date for the annual meeting has remained constant through the succeeding years.

In the operation of an educational institution, there is always some department or activity that needs to be reassessed; at the Settlement it was then the library. A tremendous number of musical scores had accumulated and many needed to be repaired and classified. Under the direction of the library committee, many volunteers worked on the music, and the scores were mended and bound in manila paper covers. All were classified under various instruments and voices, and music not needed was discarded. By November, the executive committee authorized the library committee to secure someone to catalog the library, the cost not to exceed fifty dollars. It was also approved that Violet Moore Higgins of *Town Topics* be asked to write a short story about the library with a special appeal for books. The trustees pledged that they would supply those particularly needed, if they were not procured by donation.

In May of 1919, the executive committee agreed that it would be a good idea to print a bulletin of Settlement activities to be sent to subscribers, among others. A committee was appointed, headed by Mrs. Julius Fryer, and before the end of the year, the bulletin was distributed. At the December meeting of the executive committee, it is interesting to note that Mrs. Fryer moved that the bulletin be mailed under a one-cent stamp in the future. A few random copies of this publication still remain in the files of the Settlement. Sample items from the first issue are:

> This little Bulletin makes its initial bow to the members of our Community who have helped to maintain The Cleveland Music School Settlement . . .

> The Young People's Orchestra, consisting of fifty-seven members has given two concerts at The Cleveland Museum of Art this season . . .

> A new department has been created this year in the Ensemble Class, which meets every Sunday morning, under the direction of Nathan Fryer.

The raising of money was a concern during 1919, and a garden party held in June, for which the Francis Drurys generously offered their garden, had netted three thousand two hundred and eighty dollars. In December, the Christmas caroling program, with E. A. Foote as chairman, was particularly successful and approximately three hundred groups went out. Every street in Lakewood was covered, and that district alone brought in nine hundred dollars. The total, after expenses were deducted, amounted to five thousand and sixty-six dollars, an extremely substantial sum for the time.

In September 1919, at a meeting of the executive committee, a letter of resignation from Almeda Adams was read. This letter has been lost over the years, so her reason for leaving the School cannot be verified. Conjecture suggests the following: The trustees' minutes do give the content of a letter sent to Miss Adams after her return from a leave of absence. In it she was advised, as promised, that she would be in charge of the School's chorus the following year; the music used for instruction, however, would be chosen by the heads of departments. This procedure for all the students in the School had been instituted during her absence. Miss Admas may not have cared to follow this system, because very shortly after receiving this notice, she resigned. The executive committee accepted this resignation with great regret and immediately moved to send her a letter of appreciation for all her services to the School. Certainly, she had been not only its creator, but she had been a source of inspiration to countless people.

At the last annual meeting to be held in October, a new president, Frank Muhlhauser, was elected. Toward the end of 1919, and carrying over until 1920, studies were conducted which were to lead to what was perhaps the most momentous decision ever made by the Settlement. This research was undertaken to decide whether the School should join what was then known as the Community Fund. In 1913, a new organization, the Cleveland Federation for Charity and Philanthropy, had been formed; this was the result of a decision by various welfare agencies to join together in an effort to meet community needs. In 1918, the Jewish Welfare Fund and the new Federation agreed that two groups were needed, one to raise money, the other to allocate it. Thus the Community Fund and the Welfare Federation came into existence to serve these respective functions. The name, Cleveland Federation for Charity and Philanthropy, was then dropped.

Most Clevelanders today know that the Community Fund, as it was called originally, raises money from many sources; that it is distributed to many diversified social agencies; and that this plan avoids dozens of different solicitations from business, industry, and the general public. At the time, 1919, when the trustees of the School considered joining the Community Fund, it was new and little known. (Actually, the idea for such a fund was created in Cleveland and since then has been copied all over the country.) The trustees were willing to refer the project to a committee and appointed to serve were: Francis E. Drury, Jay C. McLauchlan, Mrs. Otis S. Southworth, and the president, Frank Muhlhauser. There were, of course, varying opinions among the trustees. One, for example, thought that the Settlement should join the Community Fund and that the Fund should assume the School's entire budget; another suggested that the School should apply only for undesignated funds and should not permanently join the Welfare Federation.

At a meeting of the executive committee in November 1919, President Muhlhauser and Mr. McLauchlan, chairman of the committee to investigate the Community Fund, reported on their interviews with different officials of the Community Fund and the Welfare Federation. They had found that it was possible to join the Community Fund without joining the Welfare Federation; in that case, an organization could not be assured of receiving funds. Therefore, Mr. McLauchlan strongly advised that the Settlement join both the Fund and the Federation. The trustees had expressed some fear that they would be prevented from sponsoring benefits like the garden party or the Christmas caroling program. Because the Settlement's finances had been managed extremely well for a young organization, one can understand the reluctance on the part of board members to enter into a new relationship with the Community Fund and the Welfare Federation. However, Mr. McLauchlan emphasized his belief that becoming a member of these organizations would in no way imperil the School's strong backing in the community. Since the caroling program was so vital to the School's finances, the trustees postponed the final decision about joining until early 1920.

At the first executive committee meeting in January, the matter was discussed. Mr. McLauchlan was asked by Mr. Muhlhauser to confer with Charles E. Adams of the Community Fund in order to get a decisive answer as to just what the Fund would do for the School. By the end of January, the process of entering the Welfare Federation was explained to the executive committee, and shortly thereafter the School became a member of the Community Fund and the Welfare Federation on the following terms: the budget of the School was to be calculated from the beginning of January; the money received from the carols was to be kept separate; no more membership subscriptions were to be solicited or received, and those

which had already been sent in for 1920 were to be returned. A letter
was sent to all the former subscribers saying that funds would now
be allocated to the School by the Community Fund, but should the
Fund not continue in the future, appeals would again be made to
them.

Later in the year, letters were sent to the subscribers on two
additional occasions, reiterating that they might be asked for funds
again if the Community Fund affiliation proved to be unsuccessful.
Hindsight makes these letters rather amusing, but it is understandable
that this new relationship was considered by some to be quite
venturesome. Instead, of course, it turned out that this decision of
the board was one which helped to ensure the continuance of the
School for all the foreseeable future. Later in 1920, The Musical Arts
Association sent the Settlement fifteen hundred dollars, as it had
the year before, to sustain the School's Young People's Orchestra;
but this year the check had to be returned with an explanation of
the School's new affiliation with the Welfare Federation and the
Community Fund. It should be noted that up until the time this
history culminates (May 1974), the Community Fund has been
designated by several names: The Community Chest, United Appeal,
and United Torch Services. Thus, these names will be used inter-
changeably with that of the Welfare Federation throughout the
history, since the Federation allocated the funds raised.

Routine matters went along smoothly in 1920 — the bulletin
continued to be printed, the spring concert took place at the Duchess
Theatre as in the past, and in June, Frank Muhlhauser was re-elected
as president for another year. A thoughtful gift in memory of her
husband was received from Mrs. Albert Rees Davis, the widow of
the first president of the board. When the trustees inquired how she
wished the money to be used, she wrote:

[Letter undated; envelope stamped April 2, 1920]
I wish my gift to the Music School Settlement in
memory of Mr. Davis to be used where the trustees
feel it is most needed. They will know much better
than I about that.

I will send the Music School Settlement one
hundred dollars every April with many wishes for
its success in the wonderful work it is doing.

This money in 1920 was given to the piano department and a scholarship was awarded to Clara Sharp, whose sister, Margaret Sharp, later

played an important role in the administration of the school.

Unlooked for and certain to make a big change in the Settlement's operation was an announcement at a meeting of the executive committee in September that Walter Logan had resigned. With the School since its initial year as head of the violin department, then dean and conductor of the Young People's Symphony Orchestra, he had brought distinction and acclaim to the Settlement. His leaving marked a milestone in the history of the School. The reason for Mr. Logan's resignation was explained in the letter, dated August 25, 1920. He wrote that early in the year, Mr. Muhlhauser, president of the board, had offered him an annual salary on condition that he leave The Cleveland Orchestra. In June, when the plans for the coming year were definite, the salary designated for him fell far short of what he expected. After thinking the matter over during the summer, he felt justified in taking this step. However, in his letter, Mr. Logan also expressed his heartiest good will toward the School and wished for it every success.

To maintain the quality of the violin department, the trustees appointed as head Mrs. Frances Appleton, who had been engaged as Mr. Logan's assistant in April of 1920. The selection of a new conductor for the Orchestra was left to the orchestra committee, of which Mrs. H. P. McIntosh, Jr., was chairman. The committee very wisely chose Nathan Fryer, head of the piano department. They emphasized that the Orchestra was to be for amateur musicians only, and that it would not play in public for some time.

The Christmas caroling this year, with the consent of the Welfare Federation, was conducted most successfully under the direction of E. A. Foote and brought in four thousand six hundred and twenty-five dollars. Though it might seem repetitious to report about this annual project, its importance to the Settlement cannot be overstated. The receipts from the Christmas caroling represented more than fifteen percent of the total income.

Nineteen hundred and twenty-one saw continued work on the library; Mrs. Catherine E. Saunders, director of the school, and her assistant were cataloging the contents, and the trustees had been informed that new lighting and additional equipment would be needed. In February, some of the desired furniture had been donated, and later other necessary articles were purchased. Lighting and carpeting were installed, and with the refurnishing complete, the library had become one in which the Settlement could take pride.

In February 1921, The Musical Arts Association again demonstrated its generosity and goodwill toward the School by making it possible for a certain number of students to purchase tickets for The Cleveland Orchestra concerts at a greatly reduced rate. Many deserving students were most appreciative of this consideration. It is gratifying to report that in March, four pupils of the Settlement won scholarships to the newly established Cleveland Institute of Music, which was again a tangible evidence of the excellent teaching at the Settlement.

In May, the trustees sent a letter to the Welfare Federation giving important data about the School. It is instructive to note part of the information contained in this letter. The activities of the School included piano, violin, voice, cello, oboe, clarinet, trumpet, drums, classes in theory, solfege, chorus, dancing, and orchestral training. Pupils' recitals were given the first Sunday of each month and on every second Saturday. Fourteen thousand individual lessons had been given up to this point. There had been two faculty recitals. Musical instruction had been given to three hundred and seventy-five pupils and children showing particular talent had received specialized assistance. The budget for 1921 consisted of thirty thousand five hundred and twenty dollars in expenses and income of five thousand one hundred and thirty-three dollars from general earnings, five thousand two hundred dollars from the endowment and miscellaneous sources, and twenty-one thousand five hundred and twenty dollars from the Community Fund. The staff of thirty-five was directed by Mrs. Catherine E. Saunders. The officers were Frank Muhlhauser, president; Mrs. James Ferris, vice-president; Mrs. Andrew Squire, second vice president; Jay C. McLaughlan, third vice president; Arthur W. Pomeroy, secretary, and H. R. Drury, treasurer.

At the annual meeting in June, Mrs. Frances E. Drury was chosen as the new president. This year, 1921, The Cleveland Institute of Music, a degree-granting institution, was one year old, having been founded eight years after the Settlement. But already, the two schools were being confused, as was obvious when a check for five hundred dollars was received. The Settlement was in the process of returning the check (because of the agreement with the Community Fund), when it was informed that the contribution was intended for the Institute.

There was some question in 1921 whether the caroling program should be attempted. The Welfare Federation gave its consent for carols, provided that no money be solicited or accepted, but the trustees were of the opinion that the carols had had their day. However, Mrs. G. C. Noteman, who had so successfully managed the carols on the west side, wished to repeat the program. This was done, and a few groups sang in hospitals and for shut-ins on the east side. Though no effort was made to collect money, approximately one hundred and twenty dollars was literally thrust upon the carolers; after expenses, about eighty-five dollars was left, which was put into the School's regular expense account upon recommendation of the Community Fund.

Sad, but indicative of the fact that the members of the board were growing older, was the decision in 1921 of several longstanding trustees to retire. In January, E. A. Foote, a past president, who had given untold hours to the School from the very beginning as one of the incorporators, tendered his resignation. In September, Mrs. Otis S. Southworth, another past president, and Mrs. John S. Newberry, both exceptionally dedicated workers for the School, also felt that they should terminate their service to the Settlement. In December, a letter of resignation from a third past president, Frank Muhlhauser, was submitted. In this case, however, Mr. Muhlhauser was notified that only his resignation from the executive committee would be accepted. Apparently, he was pursuaded to stay on the board, for he was listed as a member the next year. Besides these resignations, the trustees of the School were saddened by the death of Mrs. Harvey D. Goulder, another faithful trustee who, in addition, had headed the voice department for several years. Changes come to all organizations, and conscientious trustees retire or pass away. The most compelling tribute to their service is the sustained vitality of the organization for which they volunteered. The record will show that the Settlement has been able to carry on the ideals of the early board members.

In March 1922 the trustees were again faced with the task of finding a head for the violin department; Mrs. Frances Appleton, Mr. Logan's successor, had indicated that she would be leaving at the end of the term. It was decided that the director should go to New York to search for a replacement. Upon her return, Mrs. Saunders was highly enthusiastic about Harold Berkley, who had been brought to her attention by his teacher, Franz Kneisel. The latter was the distinguished concertmaster of the Boston Symphony

Orchestra as well as founder of the renowned Kneisel Quartet. The trustees accepted the recommendation of Mrs. Saunders, and Mr. Berkley was offered the position at an annual salary of twenty-five hundred dollars. In April, the trustees learned that Nathan Fryer had volunteered to give up three hundred dollars of his salary in order to ensure Mr. Berkley's acceptance. Mr. Fryer requested only that Mr. Berkley take over some of the ensemble work. The trustees availed themselves of this generous offer and felt that the additional amount of salary was a strong inducement leading to Mr. Berkley's acceptance. Formal appreciation of Mr. Fryer's action in the interest of the School was spread upon the minutes of the executive committee.

It was reported at the annual meeting in June that two excellent performances had been given the previous month: *The Mikado* was presented by the students at the Knights of Columbus Hall, and the senior and junior orchestras participated in the annual spring concert. At this same meeting a change in the bylaws was approved, namely, that the executive committee meet only once a month in the future. The Albert Rees Davis Memorial prize money this year enabled Margaret Sharp to go to Blue Hill, Maine, for the summer to study under Willem Willeke, distinguished cellist of the famed Kneisel Quartet. Miss Sharp later was to become a devoted faculty member and registrar.

From the matters just reported, the year seemed a rather unexciting one. But with the next event, it is apparent that 1922 witnessed important changes. The trustees had known that the Settlement had only a limited time to remain at 7033 Euclid Avenue, and they were anxious to buy a home, which would give the School a permanent base for its work. At a special meeting of the trustees in October 1922, it appeared likely that this would become a reality. A suitable house had been found at 1927 East 93rd Street, the home of Mr. and Mrs. Sigmund Joseph. Terms of the purchase were outlined in the following letter which Francis E. Drury had sent to the Josephs:

[copy of undated letter in minutes]

The board of trustees of the Music School Settlement at a meeting today authorized the purchase of your property on East 93rd Street at twenty-five thousand dollars. If any agent's commission is to be paid, the Music School Settlement understands that it will assume that.

I understand from Mrs. Fryer that upon a statement in writing from me, I would be responsible for the payment to you of twenty-five thousand dollars in cash on January first, that you would require no initial deposit. I think that this is most generous of you, and I also wish to express my appreciation on behalf of Mrs. Drury, who is president of the Settlement, for the very liberal offer you have made.

I am glad to guarantee this payment to you of the above sum on the date named. The Settlement will now begin the solicitation of funds for this purpose. Whatever we may collect will be available January first and any shortage I will advance to the Settlement for the payment to you.

Sincerely,
F. E. Drury

The trustees accepted the above terms and had the secretary write a letter to Mr. Drury, as follows:

October 6, 1922

My Dear Mr. Drury,

At a special meeting of the board of trustees of the Music School Settlement held on Friday, October 6, at the School, it was unanimously voted to accept the terms for the purchase of the house belonging to Mr. and Mrs. Sigmund Joseph at 1927 East 93rd Street, to be used for the home of the Music School Settlement, as outlined in your letter to Mr. and Mrs. Joseph.

The board wishes to express to you its very great appreciation of your interest in us and of your kindness in helping us make this plan possible. The first vice president, acting in the absence of the president, appointed you chairman of the building committee.

Very truly yours,
Marion P. Stratton
Secretary pro tem

The trustees named Carl Lohmann, the treasurer, as head of a committee to begin raising the funds. At the next meeting of the executive committee in October, the plan for the fund campaign was set forth as follows:

> The executive committee and some of the trustees
> will be asked to secure this fund. Each person will
> send in a list of names of people he is willing to ask
> to contribute, these to be checked off at the School
> and returned, so that there will be no conflicts. A
> concise statement of the Music School activities will
> be written for the use of said members.

By the middle of December, less than two months later, the astonishing amount of twenty-one thousand dollars had been collected. Furthermore, V. C. Taylor & Son, realtors, had kindly offered to waive any commission. Obviously, success was in the offing. Among the larger donors were Mr. and Mrs. Francis E. Drury, Mrs. Dudley S. Blossom, Mrs. James E. Ferris, Samuel Mather, and Mrs. M. B. Otis.

Thus ended the first decade of The Cleveland Music School Settlement, with plans completed and funding available for its third home. The many details of these years make manifest the workings and objectives of the School. The period had been one of spectacular growth in the number of students and expansion in the type of instruction offered. Service such as all settlements offer — aid to the needy — had been faithfully provided, and the Settlement was now known throughout Greater Cleveland and in other parts of the country as well.

2. The Second Decade

THE SECOND DECADE STARTED OUT AUSPICIOUSLY. Trustees were gratified that the sum of twenty-six thousand one hundred and twelve dollars, which was more than enough to cover the cost of the new home, had been raised by January 1923. For the next year, nearly every meeting of the executive committee and the board was concentrated on this facility. There was much redecorating to be done, and the trustees had conceived the idea of erecting a small recital hall at the rear of the property and adding eight practice rooms. Frank B. Meade, architect and former vice president of the School, was appointed to draw up plans for these additions. The Welfare Federation advised the board that it would be difficult to raise the money for a recital hall, but the trustees were determined to go ahead; under the chairmanship of Mrs. Julius Fryer, they were able to secure contributions totaling eleven thousand one hundred and fifty dollars by June. This amount was far from sufficient, but having paid in full for the new quarters, the trustees were able to take out a mortgage for fifteen thousand dollars through the Guardian Trust Company. With financing thus arranged, construction of the additions was started and was almost complete by November.

In the meantime the main building, the former Joseph home, was being renovated. There was a break-in on one occasion, and some of the new decoration was damaged so that one room had to be redone. Other than that, all the refurbishing went smoothly. No record remains of the actual moving date, but the director, Mrs. Saunders, in giving a report on the 1923-24 School year, said that the School opened five weeks late. This would set the matriculation date in late October, and so the School must have been settled by then it its new home.

One special occurrence in 1923 is worth noting as an example of the help often given to the Settlement by outstanding Clevelanders: Dr. George Crile, the eminent surgeon and one of the founders of The Cleveland Clinic Foundation, agreed to lower his fee for an operation when his attention was directed toward the situation of the patient, a student-teacher at the School. Of routine matters, mention should be made that at the annual meeting in June, Arthur W. Pomeroy was elected president. At this same meeting, Harold Berkley's work was commended. The bulletin was still being printed, though the first issue of the year was delayed in order to included sketches and descriptions of the new home.

Because so much time had been devoted to the building project, it was December before much could be done about the caroling program, for which the Welfare Federation had again given permission. Because time was so short, the trustees had to plan for reduced caroling similar to the previous year, despite their motion to have a larger program in 1923. There were sixty groups on the west side, fewer on the east side, and voluntary contributions amounted to four hundred and fifty-two dollars. Though the monetary benefits were reduced because of the Welfare Federation's restrictions on active solicitation, the caroling program continued to bring the Settlement to the attention of many who otherwise would not have known of its existence.

The most memorable event for the School in 1924 was the opening of the new recital hall in January. To celebrate this occasion, a musical program was arranged, and the audience was addressed by President Pomeroy and the treasurer, Carl Lohmann. It is pleasant to make mention once more of the generosity to the School of a prominent Clevelander. In connection with the acquisition of the new home, Judge William C. Keough had contributed a great deal of time, and at a meeting of the executive committee in April 1924, the secretary was requested to thank the judge for his assistance.

At the annual meeting in June, Mr. Pomeroy was re-elected president for the coming year. Mrs. Saunders gave her director's report, which in this case demonstrated her perceptive understanding of the School's history, one paragraph in particular being worthy of quoting:

> Perhaps one of the greatest difficulties with us all is that we are impatient with results. It takes us a long time to learn that the best development is slow and the wide-spreading and accepting of an idea comes only when its value is deeply rooted in human consciousness. So it will always be nice to remember that, when the possibility of a Music School Settlement first presented itself to a group of Cleveland people, they chose a few attractive rooms in which

to begin the work rather than a large, fully equipped building — so that the School proved its worth and just grew and burst its walls and overflowed first into one house and then into another. Today, after twelve years of work, we find ourselves in a building of our own with this beautiful new recital hall and the addition of eight teaching rooms, well equipped and adequate for our present needs. We are deeply grateful to Mr. Lohmann for his work in connection with the building of the hall. He gave so generously of his time and thought to every detail of the work. Meantime, no stone or concrete has made our School an "institution." The welcoming, warm-hearted character of the first house has been maintained. The experimental state has long since passed, and a well-equipped and incorporate school stands among the pioneers in practical musical education for the people of this city. It's the pioneer's belief in himself and the future that makes him content to labor patiently and wait.

This year the fees for lessons were raised to fifty cents for juniors and seventy-five cents for seniors to provide for salary increases for the faculty. Also, a benefit concert was given in Mr. and Mrs. Francis E. Drury's home to raise money for the payment of the interest on the mortgage — Harold Berkley and his wife performed, and Carl Lohmann, the treasurer and a vocalist, gave a song selection — nine hundred and ten dollars was raised. New services for the community were music departments at Woodland Center and Hiram House. As usual, the caroling program at Christmas ended the year.

In 1925, an unexpected gift of five thousand dollars came to the Settlement for the building fund from a person with no formal connection to the School; this was an indication of the widespread goodwill engendered by the Settlement's activities. The bylaws and regulations were once again revised — this seems to have been almost an annual activity. However, a parliamentarian once remarked, "An organization that is continually amending its governing document is one that, undoubtedly, is moving forward continually." This was certainly true of the Settlement. At the annual meeting, Mr. Pomeroy was again re-elected president, and especially noteworthy is a quotation from a report of Mrs. Saunders in which she makes a truly prophetic statement:

> Whatever the future of the Music School Settlement
> is to be, no one with certainty can predict. But we
> can measure here today, in wide and broadening
> circles, the fruits of the vision which came to the
> men and women who received the idea, and what
> is even more, the determination to put it into action.
> If ever the musical history of Cleveland is written,
> not the least among the agencies which will be held
> up to high honor will be the Music School
> Settlement.

It is interesting, too, to refer to a project which remains something of a mystery. Recorded in the minutes of the trustees are "Vanishing Luncheons" as a means of raising money. What were they? How did they vanish? No explanation is given, but they raised one thousand four hundred and forty-two dollars, and for this reason must certainly be mentioned. The caroling program again ended the year, bringing in eight hundred and twenty-eight dollars.

Nineteen hundred and twenty-six was a comparatively uneventful year. Harold Berkley was granted a year's leave of absence to study in Europe, and Theodore Rautenberg, of New York, was hired to fill his place for the year, with the possibility of being retained as Mr. Berkley's assistant upon the latter's return. At the annual meeting in June, Mrs. Clarence L. Collens was elected as president. The item of chief interest at the meeting was the fact that an additional one thousand two hundred and seventy-nine dollars, collected from tuition, a result of the increased rates, more than balanced higher expenses. Later in the year, the tradition of a caroling program was carried on under the chairmanship of Mrs. Sterling Newell.

Nineteen hundred and twenty-seven, like 1926, was another year of more or less prosaic occurrences. Two members of the faculty, Theodore Rautenberg and Hyman Schandler, were accepted into The Cleveland Orchestra but expected to continue teaching. Mrs. Collens was re-elected president at the annual meeting, and Mrs. Saunders asked for a year's leave to rest, starting in September. The secretary at the time was to act as director during her absence. The caroling program was again undertaken, and publicity was given to it by a radio broadcast over WTAM featuring students of the Settlement. Five hundred dollars was cleared.

In 1928, circumstances of the School took an unanticipated turn when Nathan Fryer resigned as head of the piano department and proposed to the executive committee that Severin Eisenberger of Vienna be engaged as his successor. The trustees pursued Mr. Fryer's recommendation and, by fall, Mr. Eisenberger had accepted the position. Harold Berkley also resigned to continue his career in New York, and Felix Eyle was engaged to head the violin department. Interestingly, both Messrs. Eisenberger and Eyle were born in Poland and had had very distinguished careers as concert artists and teachers in Europe. Mr. Eisenberger had played with the greatest orchestras and the most famous conductors. He had taught in Berlin and Vienna, and his pupils had come from all over the world. Thus, was a particular coup for the Settlement that he came to head its piano department, as was true also of Mr. Eyle, who not only headed the violin department, but also became the assistant concertmaster of The Cleveland Orchestra. In October 1928, the trustees gave a reception for Severin Eisenberger and Felix Eyle, the two new faculty members who in succeeding years brought great distinction to the School.

A letter from the Welfare Federation, containing an omen of the coming depression, was read at a meeting of the executive committee in March 1928. The Federation asked that representatives of each agency attend a special meeting "to consider what savings can be found to help meet the emergency which has resulted from the greatly increased material relief needs following unemployment of recent months."

Normal events marked the beginning of 1929, and in June at the annual meeting, Mrs. Frank House was elected president. At a meeting of the executive committee in September, the trustees decided, after much discussion, to augment income by renting the recital hall to other organizations, a practice that has been continued through the years. At the same meeting, a decision was made concerning the policy for admitting pupils; they were to be selected from three groups: those who could pay only the regular fee of one dollar (up from the twenty-five and fifty cent fees of former years); those who were referred to the Settlement by other social agencies and who could not pay the whole fee; and those few who could pay more than the regular fee, or about one dollar and fifty cents a lesson.

In July, trustees were pleased to learn that Hilda Berkowitz, who had received all her training at the Settlement, had won the Henry

Morgenthau Scholarship at the Institute of Musical Art in New York (later merged with The Julliard School of Music). In November, a report was given to the executive committee concerning the work of the students who had been sent out to the Council of Educational Alliance, the Friendly Inn (formerly Central Friendly Inn), University Neighborhood Center, and other organizations to teach in their music departments. All these student teachers had done well and in several cases had received needed aid themselves through people connected with these groups.

By 1930, the depression was troubling all organizations, and in April, the Settlement was informed that the Welfare Federation was questioning whether the School belonged in the organization receiving Community Fund aid. At this extremely difficult time, funds were desperately needed to relieve the widespread suffering of the population. Hence, some of the Community Fund representatives thought that because the Settlement and The Cleveland Institute of Music taught music and awarded scholarships, both were in the same category; they were of the opinion that the Settlement was not sufficiently dedicated to social service.

The announcement startled but did not dismay the trustees. It presented a challenge which was met in a way that showed the dedication of the trustees and their complete confidence in the School's purposes. The whole matter lasted into 1931. The trustees paid for a survey of the work the School had done as a social service agency as well as what it could do further to increase this service. After the survey committee, composed of qualified outside persons, had made a thorough study, it suggested two plans in April 1931 to expand the service of the Settlement: (1) for a long-range plan — to bring together all the social agencies in the vicinity through their needs in music (this would involve the establishment of an advisory council); to program the study of folk songs and national characteristics of many nations, and to develop a training school for social workers and musicians; (2) for the immediate future — to continue and expand the present activities of the School while maintaining its high standards of music education; to adopt a scale to determine the economic status of the family, and to prepare a brochure to differentiate the work of the Settlement from that of the Institute of Music.

The board of trustees went on record in April 1931 as being unanimously behind these proposals. The minutes stated that the board was heartily in favor of a broad program to meet the musical needs of Cleveland's social service organizations. It also pledged its best efforts toward carrying out such a program. In June of 1931, Edward W. Garfield was elected president, and so he had the task of overseeing the implementation of the survey's suggestions.

One other recommendation made by the survey committee was that a social economist be hired in addition to a director, and it suggested Duane Ramsey for the position. Mrs. Saunders, the director since 1918, had already indicated that she would resign, and the trustees chose as her replacement Mrs. Martha Cruikshank Ramsey, who as Miss Cruikshank had worked on the survey. Mrs. Ramsey's husband, Duane, was the economist selected to make the special study throughout the summer and fall of 1931. In September of that year, after Mrs. Saunders retired, Mr. and Mrs. Ramsey took up residence at the School.

By October, the need for scholarships had accelerated, and a special meeting was called by the trustees to discuss this problem and also that of the growing deficit which had been aggravated by the expenses of the special study. One other difficult situation looming up was the extension of Chester Avenue from East 93rd to East 97th, which would put the School at the corner of the new Chester Avenue and East 93rd. The city stated that a strip of land would be taken from the School, thereby cutting a hole in the dining room of the house and slicing off the kitchen chimney! The trustees had their own study made so that proper claims for damage could be made.

In November of 1931 the question of continuing the Christmas caroling program was considered. This custom, which had raised a substantial amount for the School beginning in 1914, had been showing progressively waning interest. In view of the amount of work involved and the decreasing returns, the trustees decided it would be best to dispense with the project.

At the first meeting of the board in 1932, the trustees were presented with a most encouraging report. Though the depression was intensifying, and one might expect curtailment in the number of pupils, the enrollment in the fall had increased to six hundred and twenty-one students, which included those in the extension program. Mrs. Ramsey, the new director, pointed out that this augmentation could be attributed to the cooperation, enthusiasm, and interest of the entire faculty. Other good news was the announcement of an anonymous gift of thirty-five hundred dollars, which was to be used toward the cost of the special study. Mrs. Ramsey also made a progress report on the School's work since she had assumed her position, and it is worth quoting in part:

> The program for the present year is one of study and experimentation made at the request of the Welfare Federation of Cleveland. The study is directed on the enrichment of the present curriculum in the light of community needs. To that end we are experimenting with projects, both within the School and in cooperation with other organizations, and are doing all possible to secure and train leadership. Finally, we are attempting to construct a program which, if carried over a period, will contribute definitely to the enrichment of family life, the well-being of individuals, the service of social work and civic organizations, and the general welfare of Cleveland.

She went on to explain the adoption of a sliding scale of fees which used as a model the budget for self-supporting families developed by The Chicago Council of Social Agencies:

> A family with income sufficient only to provide simple necessities is considered eligible for a full scholarship. Those who pay less than the working price are considered as receiving part scholarships. Families whose budgets exceed the standard are asked to pay more in proportion to excess. This applies up to the point at which the fee covers the cost of teaching, supervision, and general overhead. We have not charged more than this, but rather have considered the applicant who could pay more as eligible for professional fees, and therefore not in our province.

There is much more in the report detailing all the organizations which the School was aiding by some musical activity. An interesting part of this program, one which foreshadowed a department that was established in the sixties and became prominent in the seventies was, as Mrs. Ramsey reported, the therapeutic use of music in connection with mental hygiene programs. "The Settlement," she said, "has been cooperating with the Child Guidance Clinic, Mount

Sinai Clinic, and the Psychiatric Clinic of Lakeside Hospital in planning treatment programs for unadjusted personalities.'' Mrs. Ramsey completed her report by the following comments:

> May I, in closing, pass on a thought which not now, but recently came to me in rather an overwhelming way. The occasion was a recital given by a few of our advanced students, and the Recital Hall was filled to overflowing with members of the faculty and parents who had come to hear the program of lovely substantial music. And I thought that after all in this curious world of ours, perhaps it is these things which we have been wont to think of as intangible and unreal which are the most real. Depressions may come and depressions may go, but the joy of beautiful chamber music, the graciousness of lovely songs, the companionship of a loved instrument — these things are enduring. And I profoundly hope that we shall always be permitted to share these joys with those who long for them.

In April 1932 Cleveland was host to a national conference of music supervisors. The School arranged for a tea for the visiting delegates, and since the president of this organization was much interested in the Settlement, Mr. Ramsey was asked to give a report on music in Cleveland at the conference.

An innovative proposal of Mrs. Ramsey this spring was for a summer school. She estimated that if the summer session lasted for ten weeks and could attract ninety-six pupils at the regular fee, the venture would be self-supporting. This was absolutely necessary, as there was no provision in the budget for such an undertaking, the Settlement already having a deficit in its regular program. Permission was given to Mrs. Ramsey to make plans for a summer session which proved to be completely successful, both musically and financially.

Though the board had to meet problems of deficits and other disturbing news — such as the fact that Community Fund allocations would probably be cut for all agencies the next year — still there was encouragement in the fact that the Settlement had a strong faculty. One member, Fred Rosenberg, had just received a scholarship in viola to the Curtis Institute of Music.

In June 1932 Mr. Ramsey's special study was finished; he had written it as his doctoral thesis for the Pennsylvania State University.

The study stressed particularly that The Cleveland Music School Settlement should be the center of operation for music work in all the settlements and that there should be an enlarged extension program. It propounded the idea that inasmuch as the Community Fund money would probably be decreased to all participating institutions the coming year, the Settlement should try to find other means of funding salaries and the scholarship program, possibly by foundations. As a result of the follow-up on many of the suggestions in the special study and the creative ideas of Mrs. Ramsey in implementing them, the Community Fund agreed that the School was adequately fulfilling its social service and should continue to receive Community Fund monies. Thus, the benefits of the survey far outweighed its costs.

By the fall of 1932 severe financial problems plagued all non-profit organizations as well as most of those engaged for profit. It is interesting to note how some of the Settlement's problems were met. A room in the School needed painting, and the father of a student agreed to do so *gratis;* he submitted an estimate of what it would have cost, and this amount was credited toward lessons for his son. An Oberlin graduate and a former pupil of Arthur Loesser (head of the piano department at The Cleveland Institute of Music), who had been teaching, but at the time was without a position, agreed to give fifty-two hours of teaching a month in return for a room at the School and one lesson a week with Severin Eisenberger. A graduate of Smith College and the New York School of Social Work came to Cleveland and lived at Merrick House Settlement, where she received board and lodging in exchange for supervising the music activities; she also taught at the Settlement for a salary of fifty dollars per month. Another young man, an art student, had a room at the Settlement, and in return, he made all the posters that the School needed and helped to prepare any notices that were sent out; this young art student was Charles Bartley Jeffery, who became a very prominent enamelist and teacher.

Despite all these expedients, a special meeting of the trustees had to be called in November. Funds were running out, and unless more money was forthcoming, the School would have to suspend operations at the end of November and remain closed through the month of December. The board decided to borrow two hundred and fifty dollars from the building fund to keep the School functioning until December 17th. It remained open until then, but the faculty received no salary for the latter part of the month. That they met the situation with a wonderful spirit of understanding and cooperation speaks well for the personnel and their dedication to the School.

In the throes of overcoming very difficult financial problems, the second ten-year period of The Cleveland Music School Settlement was concluded.

3. Depression Years and a New Home

IT IS SELF-EVIDENT that this third decade of the School's existence started under dark clouds. By 1933, the country was in an economic depression. Not only had businesses and factories failed and unemployment reached gigantic proportions, but there was a bank holiday in Cleveland, which left the Settlement without funds for operation. Moreover, despite the five hundred and nineteen students enrolled, there was a deficit of nine hundred dollars. It is not necessary to go into the details of this discouraging situation; let it suffice to say that Edward W. Garfield, the president of the board, must be given the eternal gratitude of the School. He went out by himself, quietly soliciting funds to keep the School from closing down entirely.

That is not to say that the School in these years could expand and carry on as it might have desired; all through the 1930s it was, as were most people and organizations, short of funds. Instruments which were wearing out could not be replaced. In fact, when pianos were needed, committees had to search very hard in order to find good ones at affordable sums. At a meeting of the trustees in January 1934, the chairman of the house committee reported with some discouragement, "the committee is still looking for a bargain in a grand piano." The school year itself had to be curtailed and there was never enough money for scholarships as more and more students required financial assistance. In April of 1935, Severin Eisenberger, head of the piano department, and Felix Eyle, head of the violin department, offered to give a benefit sonata recital to raise money for scholarships. This took place in May, and another benefit recital by Felix Eyle was given in November in Severance Chamber Music Hall.

During these years, too, as the numbers of unemployed persons increased drastically, efforts were made to help fill their idle days and hours. There was, for example, the University Neighborhood Center Program for the unemployed, with which the Settlement cooperated. As its contribution to this program, according to the director's report of January 1934, the School offered a music appreciation class, a singing class for mixed voices, and an open house every Friday evening with varied entertainment including informal music, folk music, and student recitals.

The director of the School reported to the trustees in June 1935 and voiced the problem of the unemployed again when she said:

> The enlarged leisure which has come to many is creating a need for new uses of this "living time" and is increasing our responsibility to provide music opportunity for the constructive use and not the abuse of leisure. To meet these needs, more thought must be given to the social aspect of music and the allied arts and every effort made to develop the resources at hand. More opportunity must be made available for large and small groups in singing and ensemble playing.

By April 1936 the director could report:

> In the total number of individuals coming to the Settlement for group work, those over eighteen years of age are about forty percent of the total number. . . . This shows a decided increase in the number of adults over the figures of two years ago. The evident reasons for this are unemployment and increasing desire of amateurs to actually perform and not only to listen to music.

During those years and up to September 1940 the National Youth Association, a federal organization of the depression, was of great help. Students were paid on an hourly basis — some had office duties, others did cleaning. The School could hardly have maintained its premises in good order in these years without this assistance from the government.

In June 1933 Mrs. Ramsey, the director, and her husband, who had led the School into new fields of extension work resigned because of their wish to return to New York. The trustees endeavored to persuade them to continue but were not successful. In consequence, the Settlement was without a permanent director for several months until November 1933, when Miss Emily McCallip was named to the post. Thoroughly in sympathy with the ideals of the School, she came from Philadelphia where from 1916 to 1924 she had been with the Settlement Music School and for the following eight years with the

Curtis Institute of Music.

Since The Cleveland Music School Settlement now collaborated with the settlement houses of the city in their music programs, there was a need for more teachers with the background necessary for this work. Miss McCallip had pointed out as early as January 1934 the efforts of the School to fill idle days and hours for the unemployed, and again referred to the problem at the annual meeting of the board in June 1935. She told the trustees at this same meeting of the need for teachers:

> One of the more important problems for the coming year, I believe, will be the selection and training of leaders to carry on not only in Cleveland, but throughout the country. It is an acknowledged fact and recognized by the National Federation of Settlements in Montreal last week, that there is no better place to be found for such training at the present moment than in Cleveland. This is due to the opportunities offered at Western Reserve University (School of Social Science, School of Education, and Music Department), the unusual advantages for the study of characteristics and traditions of the many nationalities living here, the ten settlements available as a training field, and The Cleveland Music School Settlement as an established center.

By January 1936, such a program had been organizd for those interested in teaching music in settlements and other social agencies. It was a two-hour course of sixteen weeks in two sections, the first a seminar, the second a lecture giving the background of music and nationalistic culture. By the end of 1937, Miss McCallip stated that the leadership training course was proving of great benefit to those teaching in this and other settlements.

At the same meeting in June 1935, the director had also recommended the hiring of a case worker or family visitor. "Even with the help of three board members and the teachers," she said, "visits to homes of pupils have been very few, so that this has become one our weakest points." By June of 1936, a case worker had been hired.

A policy adopted during the 1930s requiring new teachers to give one recital a year provided more faculty recitals for the public. Many of the teachers had already been doing this, Severin Eisenberger and Felix Eyle being examples; Mr. Eisenberger appeared very often also as a soloist with The Cleveland Orchestra. While music critics were most laudatory about faculty members' performances in other locales for which there was a charge, Settlement audiences were privileged to hear the same artists at no cost. The occasions were indeed fulfilling the hopes of the founders and providing bright spots for music lovers in the depression years. There were other happy events more personal to the School, such as a tea given in honor of Emma Eames, who in 1914 had helped the School immensely by her benefit concert and who was now visiting Cleveland. One occurrence not so felicitious was the resignation of Severin Eisenberger, who accepted a position at the Cincinnati Conservatory of Music.

The year 1937 marked the silver anniversary of the School. The manner in which it was celebrated was fitting for these depression years. First, the board of trustees gave a luncheon in September 1937, at the Mid-Day Club, for the faculty who had carried on despite cuts in salaries and other hardships. Then, in October, through the courtesy of Mrs. Edward Bok of Philadelphia, the School arranged a concert by the Curtis String Quartet to be given in the Severance Chamber Music Hall as a benefit for the Settlement. This world-renowned quartet received high praise for the excellence of its playing from all Cleveland critics, and it also publicized the Settlement, whose sponsorship was mentioned in every reference to the concert. Importantly, this performance added to the scholarship monies of the School. The evening following the concert, the Curtis Quartet consented to perform at the School for the students. The final event in honor of the anniversary was another benefit concert at Severance Hall in November by the noted violinist, Samuel Dushkin; he had spent much time with Igor Stravinsky and was well known to Clevelanders through his marriage to the daughter of Louis Rorimer, a prominent Clevelander. A *Cleveland Plain Dealer* headline proclaimed that "Cleveland Society Prepares to Make Dushkin Violin Recital Gala Affair on Thursday." A social occasion it was, as well as a fine concert and another boost for scholarships.

As 1938 dawned, it was not immediately evident that the year would be a banner one for the School. The matter of the Chester extension had been lurking in the background since 1931, and now the actual work was soon to start. The city had said it would pay one thousand dollars for damage to the Settlement's building, an amount the trustees protested. Not only would the property be less valuable, but it would be assessed an additional four thousand dollars to six thousand dollars in improvement taxes. Moreover, by 1937 the neighborhood was deteriorating, and it was rumored that the East 93rd Street location was becoming a "red light" district. After a careful analysis of the situation, the president of the board, Edward W. Garfield, listed all the disadvantages of remaining in this location: the house would be mutilated by the slicing off of part of the property; some rooms of the house and the recital hall would be so near the street that traffic noise would make them unusable unless very expensive sound-proofing was installed; the fire department expected to ban parking on East 93rd Street and part of Chester Avenue after the extension, and there would be added "improvement" taxes.

As had happened several times in the past when the School needed larger quarters, dedicated trustees made it possible to move. This time, another happy circumstance arose. The Edmund S. Burke, Jr., house on Magnolia Drive (the house of the good war garden of 1918) was for sale; largely through conversations between Edward W. Garfield and Mr. Burke, it was offered to the School for the nominal sum of twenty-five thousand dollars. The acquisition was hotly debated at a board meeting, but trustee Mrs. Thomas Munro spoke up very strongly in favor of the purchase and urged the board not to be shortsighted in making a decision. Her words were effective, for after carefully going over the house and considering its favorable location near Severance Hall, The Cleveland Museum of Art, and Western Reserve University, as well as its proximity to public transportation on Wade Park, Euclid Avenue, and East 105th Street, the trustees felt that they had found an ideal home. Consultation with the Welfare Federation followed, and then, at a meeting of the board in June 1938, it was agreed to buy the property. With this acquisition, the School now had the most outstanding quarters of any community music school in the country.

The house, located as it was among those of the city's leading families — the Wades, Hannas, Mathers, and Chisholms — was built in 1910 at a reputed cost of three hundred thousand dollars. It was designed by J. Milton Dyer in the style of the fine English manor houses. Many of its features — double glass windows, brass plumbing, and pull-down window screens — were ahead of the times. The house contained carved ceilings and paneled walls in the main rooms; the walnut wood of the library was graced by especially lovely and ornate carving. Floors throughout the home were of wood parquet with interesting and varied designs; fireplaces were faced with beautiful marble, and in the drawing room hung dazzling rock crystal chandeliers. There was even a pipe organ. A few years later, some of the original furniture, including the carved Jacobean chairs and the huge oak table in the foyer, was given to the Settlement by Mrs. Edmund S. Burke, Jr. The rare embellishments of the house were preserved and have provided over the years an inspiring background for music and its practitioners, both professional and student. The School moved into this great forty-two room mansion in August of 1938. It took several months to procure furniture by gift and loan, so that the opening and the dedication did not occur until October. A large number of music lovers and social service workers of the city attended.

In June of 1938, not too long before its big move, the School had organized a parents group in response to many requests. It soon grew to include not only parents, but also young adults studying at the Settlement, and became known as the Parent-Adult Organization. The attendance by its members at School lectures on different musical subjects made for greater cooperation and understanding between them and the faculty. Because of this success, the trustees agreed to include one of the organization's officers in an ex-officio capacity on the board.

There was also another new project which again was an indication of the Settlement's forward-looking outlook. In 1937, the School had entered into an experiment with an organization called Garfield House, the purpose of which was to help correct the speech of children with hearing problems through the use of singing. The voice department was in charge of the Settlement's part of the experiment, and by June 1939 the trustees for Garfield House expressed gratitude for its participation in the two-year research program to prove the value of music in the education of the hard-of-hearing children. The results had been more positive than had even been anticipated. In May 1940 the trustees of Garfield House again acknowledged the support of the Settlement and especially commended the work of Marie Fritzinger Butler (Mrs. John), head of the department of social music. Interestingly, "social" as used then connoted ensemble singing.

To read the music columns in the newspapers all through the 1930s is to learn how fortunate Cleveland was in its calendar of musical events. The Settlement's faculty recitals were among the best when Severin Eisenberger and Felix Eyle appeared; when Leonard Rose, the brilliant twenty-one-year-old principal cellist of The Cleveland Orchestra, made his recital debut at the School; and when Jacques Posell, double bassist, and pianist Leon Machan, both of The Cleveland Orchestra, performed together. The list could go on and on, but it does give some idea of the faculty members' high degree of excellence and the quality of musical programs that the Settlement made available to the people of the community without charge.

In June of 1939, Dr. Myron S. Schaeffer, head of the theory department, and his wife, a member of the piano faculty, were granted a year's leave of absence for study in Europe. Dr. Schaeffer had been awarded a fellowship by the Belgian-American educational committee. He returned to Cleveland in May 1940 and asked for another year's leave, even though World War II had already started. However, Dr. Schaeffer had to leave Belgium less than a month after his arrival because of the German invasion. A newspaper account of the time (*Cleveland Plain Dealer,* March 3, 1939), says:

> Other Clevelanders who were relating their experiences in leaving the war zone today included Dr. Myron S. Schaeffer, instructor in music at Western Reserve University and The Cleveland Music School Settlement, and his wife who went to Brussels, Belgium, with their four-year-old son less than a month ago.
>
> "We stopped at England where we were held up for nine hours while Britain confiscated a shipment of aluminum scheduled for Germany," said Dr. Schaeffer in describing the homeward trip on the *Manhattan.* "Then we dropped over to Cork for the express purpose of picking up Postmaster General James A. Farley."
>
> "We knew about the *Athenia* and many of the passengers were nervous and hysterical," he continued. "One young woman became insane and had to be confined in the ship's infirmary."

There were several exciting days at the Settlement in 1940, when Leopold Stokowski came to Cleveland to audition thirty-three young musicians for the one hundred-piece youth symphony with which the celebrated maestro expected to tour South America. During the sessions, Mr. Stokowski had an altercation with some of the newspaper reporters when they attempted to take his picture against his wishes. This "tempest in a teapot" was written up melodramatically in the newspapers, so inadvertently the Settlement received even greater publicity from the visit of the maestro than had been anticipated.

In the fall of 1940, there was a new head of the piano department in the person of Boris Goldovsky. Having completed his piano studies at the Franz Liszt Academy in Budapest, he toured as a concert artist in Europe for several years and came to the United States to study conducting with Fritz Reiner at the Curtis Institute of Music. Subsequently, he was invited by Artur Rodzinski, then music director of The Cleveland Orchestra, to help prepare the opera productions at Severance Hall. Mr. Goldovsky was a remarkable musician, having been appointed conductor of both the Orchestra's Philharmonic Chorus and the Singers Club, as well as director of the opera department at The Cleveland Institute of Music. With the very active role that he took in the city's musical life, he was a great addition to the faculty of the Settlement. Also appointed as head of a new department of accompanying was Leon Machan, the official pianist of The Cleveland Orchestra. Individual voice lessons were discontinued at this time, as interest had waned, but there were classes for group singing.

In 1941, the School continued adding to its accomplishments, when more than a dozen of its advanced students won scholarships to conservatories, colleges, and universities. In the fall, a concert given by Leonard Rose and Boris Goldovsky attracted an audience that overflowed from the recital hall into the corridors, the vestibule, and up the stairs. Also of interest, The Cleveland Orchestra played a composition by Herbert Haufrecht, who in earlier years had studied at the School with Nathan Fryer.

With the attack on Pearl Harbor on December 7, 1941, the Settlement was called upon to provide new services. By February, the office of civilian defense asked the School to arrange a song-leaders training course; it was thought that group singing would be helpful in keeping up morale. By April, three of the trustees had to resign, as various defense duties kept them too busy to attend meetings. In June, it was decided to schedule one of the summer recitals in late morning, so defense workers of an afternoon or evening shift could attend. In addition to music furnished by the School to aid the war effort, the School now had faculty and staff members active in the air warden service, the blood donors group, the civilian defense, and first aid classes. Closer to the war were twenty-seven of the School personnel known to be in the armed forces. In her annual report of this year, 1942 Miss McCallip said:

> For us, too, the war time is bringing rapid changes in a swiftly accelerating pace — so rapid, that it is impossible to plan ahead as we have been accustomed to this last nine years. It is evident, that any creative ideas which come to us for development, must wait until such time as they can be materialized. We are being challenged — but challenge means opportunity. For the duration, the manner in which we carry on, must necessarily be conceived on a short range basis, rather than on a long range plan. There are those in high places who do not see the need of maintaining and developing our cultural institutions. They have not yet visioned the real value of art and education in such times as these — not even with the proven experiences in England and Russia to point the way. Fortunately, there is no sign yet that this part of our life in the United States of America will be destroyed either by wartime restrictions or by the inertia of the people themselves.

That the School did maintain its work and essay into even greater service becomes obvious as its history unfolds into the fourth decade.

4. War Years and Aftermath

DESPITE THE VICISSITUDES brought about by the war; the Settlement made brave efforts to maintain a near normal schedule as well as to do its part for the war effort. More and more of the faculty, staff, and older students were taken into the armed forces, and a number of the faculty entered defense plants, some working on a night shift and teaching during the day. Board president Garfield was absent for a period while taking an army orientation course for civilians at Fort Leavenworth, Kansas. Boris Goldovsky, piano department head, left the Settlement in 1942 for Boston to be in charge of the opera department at the New England Conservatory of Music and the piano department of the Longy School of Music.

Though the faculty was changed and students were leaving, the programs at the School continued to be of high caliber. In March 1943, two chamber music recitals drew capacity crowds, and one featured an unusual work, the *Trumpet Septet* by Vincent D'Indy. In April, a concert was given on a Sunday afternoon honoring the faculty and students who were in the armed forces. Their parents and friends were invited, and the musical program was given by former faculty Walter Cerveny, a violinist, and Harold Fink, a pianist, both stationed in Cleveland with the coast guard, and Anthony Sophos, cellist in The Cleveland Orchestra, who expected to be inducted into the army. At this concert, community singing took place as well as the dedication of a roll of honor for the sixty-nine in the service. Another well-reviewed program was "Music for Old and Modern Flute" played by Maurice Sharp, faculty member and first flute of The Cleveland Orchestra. All these and other programs drew good audiences and in a sense contributed to the war effort by keeping up morale. Mr. Garfield suggested this when he said at the annual meeting in June 1943:

> Many of the people who have come to these recitals
> and other events of the season have found our house
> to be a grateful haven from the many problems and
> difficulties of life in war time.

Several other events that took place in the spring of 1943 should be mentioned. A surprise party with one hundred and fifty guests was given in March for Mrs. Adella Prentiss Hughes, whose sympathetic response to Almeda Adams's suggestion had resulted in the Settlement's founding. In May, the School lost by resignation Leonard Rose, head of the cello department, who left The Cleveland Orchestra to become principal cellist of the New York Philharmonic. By June, the service roll had increased to eighty-four, and the adult registration of the term just ended had decreased fifty percent. Fortunately, there was a notable increase in the number of children enrolled. In spite of the fact that so many faculty members had to be replaced because of induction into the service, there continued to be major accomplishments by Settlement students. Two of the senior students had joined The Cleveland Orchestra, and others had won scholarships to Peabody Institute of Music; Berkshire Music School; Western Reserve University; Oberlin College; the Curtis Institute of Music; The Cleveland Institute of Music; and Longy School of Music.

In this war year, too, the summer school was held again, which was quite an achievement considering that there was gasoline rationing. It had first been tried in 1932 but had to be discontinued after two years because of the depression. Commenced again in 1935, it had been kept going and the war, unlike the depression, did not stop its being carried on in the forties. In summing up this summer term of 1943, the assistant director of the School, Louise Palmer Walker, commented: "I know the other faculty members join me in feeling that these six weeks are well spent, as students are out of regular school and have time for concentrated music study."

A highlight of the summer session in 1943 was an open-air courtyard concert at the back of the School. The first one had been given in 1941, when, rather unexpectedly, the acoustics had proved to be unusually good. The concert in 1943 featured a string quartet composed of former students of the Settlement who at this time were in The Cleveland Orchestra: Joseph Koch, Vincent Greicius, Fred Rosenberg, and Anthony Sophos (still waiting to be inducted into the service). Herbert Elwell, music critic of the *Cleveland Plain Dealer,* said: "Amidst the twittering of the robins and the strident notes of the blue jays, a beautiful concert of Mozart and Haydn and other quartets was heard."

It is perhaps well to speak now of the musicianship classes which had been started by the School in 1938. Originally, they were for pre-school children under six, but the demand for this type of training became so great that, by 1943, there were classes not only for pre-school children but also for children of kindergarten and first-grade age as well as for still older students up to thirteen years. The object of the musicianship instruction was to give a background for instrumental study. Fundamentals such as rhythm, note-reading, ear-training, and dancing broadened the music experience of these young people, and a semester of musicianship was given before any instrument study was attempted. However, by the next year, 1944, in accord with the School's propensity for experiment, this approach was changed to enable children nine years of age and over to study an instrument after only a month of musicianship. The new system proved to be successful. After the musicianship classes, the pupils graduated into the theory of music course, and Mrs. John Butler, head of this work, could truthfully state:

> Our students are not robots and infant prodigies
> who can play a pretty tune. They are well-grounded
> in the fundamentals of a musicianly and artistic
> approach to the study of music; children who know
> intellectually as well as emotionally what music
> study really means.

The Settlement lost a great friend when former president Mrs. Francis E. Drury died in 1943. Over the years, she and her husband had been munificent benefactors of the Settlement, and her demise ended a trust agreement which had been formalized in 1937. The School received securities, stocks, and bonds which by the terms of the trust agreement could either be converted into cash to pay any indebtedness or held in the interest of the School. The securities were all held until 1944, when the trustees decided to use the proceeds from the sale of part of them to pay off the mortgage. Thus, Mr. Garfield could announce at the annual meeting in June of 1944 that, for the first time since 1923, the School was entirely free of debt. He also told the Board that the property on East 93rd Street had been sold, and that after its mortgage and expenses had been paid, thirty-eight hundred dollars had been deposited in a special account.

This annual meeting included an interesting report of three years' work by Dorothea Doig. She had been giving tests, the Seashore Measure of Musical Talent, to almost three hundred pupils of the School in an endeavor to determine the musical capacity of each student. This testing was again one more example of the School's desire to adopt the newest methods. It was found that the results in general agreed with the teachers' estimates of the pupils' ability. Miss Doig then suggested that the tests might be given to those on the waiting list to determine which ones should be given preference for entrance. Also at this meeting, an account was given by a representative of the Parent-Adult Organization concerning the speakers during the year. Among them had been the well-known member of Cleveland's intellectual community, Dr. Joseph Remenyi, a professor at Western Reserve University; he had given a talk for the trustees in 1940, and some years later, a series of comparative arts lectures for faculty, staff, and the general public. Dr. Remenyi had served as a board member, and his talks and service as a trustee were representative of the help given the Settlement by outstanding citizens.

The summer session of 1944 largely financed itself, but it was found that there were still many students whose fees could not be increased. From interviews that fall, the administration learned that there were countless families who were still very poor and that not all who were working in the factories made high wages. Pupils continued to win scholarships and the numbers on the honor roll increased.

The end of World War II in 1945 brought vital changes to the Settlement and the country. A great loss for the School were three resignations: Felix Eyle, head of the violin department for seventeen years, who left both the School and his position as assistant concertmaster of The Cleveland Orchestra to become concertmaster of the Metropolitan Opera Orchestra; Maurice Sharp, head of the flute department, who temporarily departed from The Cleveland Orchestra to go to New York; and Emily McCallip, now Mrs. Lawrence Adler, who had managed the Settlement so ably for twelve years, wished to retire. To fill Mrs. Adler's place, the trustees appointed Louise Palmer Walker as director. Having been assistant director for several years and a valuable member of the violin faculty, Miss Walker was well-qualified to carry on for Mrs. Adler. Both had come originally from the Curtis Institute of Music.

Before leaving, Mrs. Adler reported to the trustees at the annual meeting in June and listed some of the important events of late 1944 and the first half of 1945. Quoting Mrs. Adler:

> Although there have been no extraordinary changes
> and events at the Settlement this year, such as

moving into this wonderful house, starting the Parent-Adult Organization, engaging a part-time case worker, including a representative from the faculty and the Parent-Adult Organization on the board of trustees, yet in many ways this has been one of the most successful years in the history of the Settlement.

The attendance has been quite remarkable. It was well nigh perfect during the hottest days of the summer school and during the coldest and stormiest days of the winter. The student recitals have improved in program, attendance, and general interest. . . .

The lesson fees have increased beyond any expectations of five years ago (an increase of fourteen hundred dollars this year). . . .

This past season our students have won scholarships to The Cleveland Institute of Music, Eastman School of Music, Julliard School, Oberlin Conservatory of Music, and Western Reserve University in the School of Education. . . .

In addition, students have been engaged on a regular professional basis by the following orchestras: Kansas City Symphony (viola); Columbus Symphony (bassoon, cello, and violin); Houston Symphony (violin, cello, and oboe); New York City Summer Stadium Concerts (violin and cello). . . .

At this 1945 annual meeting, an account was given of an in-house survey that had been made during the year. The rather interesting results showed, among other statistical information, that piano study was the most popular with the students; next came musicianship classes, followed by violin study. It also revealed that the work engaged in by the fathers of the students covered nearly all known occupations, ranging from laborers and truck drivers to physicians and attorneys.

VJ Day, marking the end of World War II, was celebrated on September 2, 1945, and, in reviewing these war years, the School could now count more than two hundred of its former students and personnel who had served in the armed forces. A very fine tribute to the Settlement was contained in a letter which had come during those years from a radarman, first class, serving in the South Pacific; the writer was Thomas J. Sargous, the future husband of registrar Flora Wayne. The letter read, in part:

> You at the Settlement are doing a most important job. We out here know, because we can readily see what it is that is the most important asset a man can have in this messy business. It is the fact that he maintains a will to live, and that will is prompted by a strong, firm hope for the future built on a foundation of what has gone on before in his life. If he has had some small measure of acquaintance with the things the Settlement advocates — if you have had a hand in instilling thoughts far from sordidness, prejudice, and war, please do feel that you have, and are helping win the war.

The time from the war's end and throughout 1946 was a period of re-adjustment to peace-time conditions as well as re-evaluation of the aims, accomplishments, and future plans of the Settlement. The re-evaluation, in this instance, part of a Settlement study, is a function which the School still carries on from time to time. In such a study (later named self-study), the aims of the School are reviewed and an examination is made whether they have been accomplished; also, new objectives of the School are proposed and improvements in procedure recommended. The study this particular year concluded that most of the purposes of the School were being implemented. But it went on to suggest that the School should continue to maintain the high quality of its instruction; that its teachers should be trained to be sensitive to students' behavior which might be symptomatic of emotional difficulties, and finally, that the board of trustees and administrative staff of the School should endeavor to get all possible information concerning state or national legislation which might affect the music community. The following is a list of what the School wanted to accomplish:

(a) to engage additional faculty in order to use fully the facilities of the present building;

(b) to provide adequate salaries for the staff;

(c) to develop more library facilities for the students;

(d) to have a person of national reputation as head

of the piano department;

(e) to re-instate individual voice lessons;

(f) to add instruction in trombone and French horn, and,

(g) to give a larger number of talented students from families at lower incomes the opportunity for more specialized training.

A great many veterans, who had been former students, visited the School as soon as they returned home. Within one hour, for example, a boy just back from the Pacific came in, followed closely by a veteran from Germany. Some of the veterans immediately enrolled again at the Settlement; others came for advice concerning their study elsewhere. The personnel of the School endeavored to counsel these former students and to help them in being admitted to the schools of their choice. The Settlement's most gratifying achievement in this respect was to obtain entrance for Walter Cerveny to the Yale School of Music, after admissions were closed.

In other ways, too, the Settlement assisted in this transitional period. The Parent-Adult Organization sponsored a lecture by Colonel Robert H. Owens, supervisor of veterans' education; he gave useful advice to parents whose children, returning from the service, were desirous of continuing their schooling under the GI bill. The trustees gave a homecoming reception for the servicemen and their families. In June, the annual courtyard concert was a tribute to those who had been in the service. Fourteen returned veterans played in the orchestra, and the second part of the program was a memorial to the five students who had given their lives. These five young men were further commemorated by scholarships given in their names for the instruments they had studied at the School: Pvt. William Deeter, oboe; Lt. Marvin Goldston, trumpet; Pfc. Henry Golebiewski, cello; Pfc. Edward Kuznik, piano; and Pvt. Edward Williams, piano. Former faculty who had been in the service returned to their posts, and these included Fred Rosenberg, violin; Martin Heylman, flute; and Steve Matyi, oboe. Maurice Sharp, who had resigned in 1945, also returned as head of the flute department and as first flute of The Cleveland Orchestra.

Enrollment in 1946 went up to one thousand seven hundred and twenty-one, as compared to nine hundred and seventeen for 1945, and summer school registration rose from four hundred and forty-two to five hundred and twelve. The year was marked by a number of special events, among them: a recital by Charles Joseph, violinist from the Curtis Institute of Music, and another by Patricia Marshall of the Oberlin Conservatory of Music. Receptions were held for former distinguished faculty members: Felix Eyle on a visit here from New York City and Boris Goldovsky from Boston. The registrar, Flora Wayne, had become Mrs. Thomas Sargous, and she and her husband were also honored by a reception. In addition, the School re-instated an orchestra of its own called the Settlement Chamber Orchestra. The former senior orchestra of the Settlement had been merged in 1936 with that of Western Reserve University.

At this time, 1946, several special honors came to the School. Melvin Ritter, a former violin student who had played many concerts in Europe for both the Army and civilians during his military service, was selected by the National Music League in New York as one of the young artists it would launch on a concert career; Louise Palmer Walker, the director of the School, was asked to serve on the executive committee of the National Guild of Community Music Schools; fifty-two Settlement students received first or second rating in the public school music contests which were held under the auspices of the Cleveland board of education.

Three events of importance occurred in 1947: plans were going ahead for a new library to be housed in the coach house; Josef Gingold, concertmaster of The Cleveland Orchestra, was appointed head of the violin department, and Louise Palmer Walker, the director, was forced by ill health to take an indefinite leave of absence. There were lesser matters — the Parent-Adult Organization became the Almeda Adams Club (Miss Adams herself attended several of the group's meetings and in a talk to the members shared with them many memories of the past); now that the war was over and new equipment available, the Settlement was able to purchase three Steinway grand pianos through a grant from the Kulas Foundation.

Miss Walker's health did not improve sufficiently for her to reassume her duties at the Settlement, and she retired permanently. Howard Whittaker, a candidate for her position, was interviewed by three trustees, who comprised the search committee: Russell V. Morgan, head of the music department of the Cleveland board of education; Dr. Arthur Shepherd, head of the music department at Western Reserve University, former assistant conductor of The Cleveland Orchestra, and a distinguished composer, and Mrs.

Thomas Munro, a former student of Josef Hofmann at the Curtis Institute of Music. Mrs. Munro was so favorably impressed by Mr. Whittaker's credentials and the many things he had already accomplished, though still in his twenties, that after the interview, she telephoned the president immediately, highly recommending him. The other trustees and the president concurred with Mrs. Munro, and in February of 1948, Mr. Whittaker was appointed acting director; eight months later he was made director, the first male to occupy this position in the thirty-six years since the School was founded. Mr. Whittaker was a 1943 graduate of The Cleveland Institute of Music. After two and a half years in the army, he had entered the Oberlin Conservatory of Music and obtained a master's degree. This was followed by additional graduate work at the Eastman School of Music and study of composition with Herbert Elwell.

As the years have passed, it has become evident that no choice of a director at that time could have been more propitious for the welfare of the School. Mr. Whittaker's philosophy of teaching was that music education should contribute to the students' freedom of expression, and that discipline was one of the joys and qualifications of art. He also placed great emphasis on group participation — classes, chorus, ensembles, orchestras—which enabled the students to share musical experiences with others, rather than just to take a private lesson a week. To reach these goals, Mr. Whittaker undertook a reorganization of all departments and the curriculum to insure well-coordinated and interrelated departments; he established a certificate of accomplishment for students who had completed the pre-conservatory level of requirements in order to give them a goal and to stimulate more community interest in the School; and he prescribed new procedures for auditioning, examinations, and recitals.

The theory department was now under Mr. Whittaker's direction. He organized it into a preparatory group division for children six to eleven years of age; a four-year program for pupils twelve to seventeen years; adult theory classes which paralleled standard conservatory requirements; and finally, for those who possessed the necessary background, orchestration and composition on an individual basis. To encourage group work a student string quartet and a string orchestra were formed, and these two ensembles also helped to serve the community by giving numerous performances.

Another valuable suggestion of Mr. Whittaker's was that a publicity committee of trustees be appointed to help prepare a catalogue comparable to those issued by other music school settlements. He also arranged interesting programs. Herbert Elwell, music critic of the *Cleveland Plain Dealer,* commented (April 26, 1948): "This faculty concert, the first given at the Settlement since Howard Whittaker took over the direction of the School, fairly sparkled with novelties ably presented. . . ." By the end of 1948, Mr. Garfield, the president of the board, could point with pride to the well-organized departments, planned with the thought in mind that the School was both a settlement and a music school, and to the fact that the distinguished concert pianist and teacher, Leonard Shure, had been named head of the piano department.

The appointment to this position of a person with a national reputation had been strongly advised in the Settlement study of 1946. With Leonard Shure, the School exceeded this directive; his concert tours had already brought him international acclaim. Born in Los Angeles, he had concertized extensively in this country before going to Berlin, Germany, at the age of fourteen to study with Arthur Schnabel. From 1927 to 1933 as Schnabel's first assistant he played many concerts throughout Europe. Returning to the United States in 1933, he taught at the New England Conservatory, the Longy School of Music, and the Mannes Music School; for a time he was the acting head of the piano department at The Cleveland Institute of Music. During these years he performed as soloist with many orchestras and as assisting artist with numerous chamber music ensembles.

In May 1949 the School presented a faculty recital of Brahms sonatas played by Josef Gingold and Leonard Shure at Severance Chamber Music Hall. It had been rightly judged, as Arthur Loesser, music critic of *The Cleveland Press* observed, that the recital hall of the School would be too small for the crowd expected. Even the chamber music hall proved to be inadequate; hundreds had to be turned away. All faculty recitals were presented without charge, and this concert attracted many students in addition to the regular patrons. The reviews were most favorable. Elmore Bacon, the *Cleveland News* music critic, remarked: "We are indebted to Director Howard Whittaker, of the Settlement School, for providing such a treat and in such pleasant surroundings."

Through the years, the Settlement has often cooperated with other institutions in presenting noteworthy events, and in 1949 it joined with Western Reserve University in presenting a series of six Bach concerts, which carried over into 1950. The series commemorated the two-hundredth anniversary of the composer's death; its purpose was stated in the various programs as follows:

> Western Reserve University and The Cleveland Music School Settlement are presenting three concerts in an effort to acquaint the musical public with a number of the less frequently heard instrumental works of Johann Sebastian Bach. During the present scholastic year and that which follows, we shall present the faculty and students from both institutions as soloists.
>
> The works of an intimate nature will be given in the Settlement recital hall, while those which are more orchestral in scope will be played in Harkness Chapel on the campus of Western Reserve University.

Another cooperative event was a joint venture with Karamu House for the opening of its theatre. In December 1949 these two institutions produced Stravinsky's ballet suite, *The Soldier's Tale,* with Karamu dancers, and Menotti's opera, *The Medium,* which featured Dr. Zelma George (later to become a Settlement advisory trustee). Howard Whittaker conducted, and Dr. Benno Frank of Karamu Theatre and also director of the opera workshop at the Settlement, directed the stage production. The orchestra consisted of fifteen faculty members, all of whom were Cleveland Orchestra members, and seven advanced students.

An important "first" for the Settlement was the publication of the catalogue which Mr. Whittaker had recommended; it was distributed to the trustees in April 1949, as well as to Almeda Adams, numerous colleges, newspapers, and other settlement agencies. An attractive publication, the cover had been designed by Alfred Howell, an advisory trustee and head of the art department of the Cleveland public schools. The catalogue included a short history of the School, concise biographies of the former directors, a note about the Almeda Adams Club, as well as information about faculty, courses, and admission requirements.

Particularly deserving of record in 1949: Howard Whittaker was elected president of the National Guild of Community Music

Schools, and his seventeen-year-old student, Gerald Humel, won a first prize for composition in the annual scholastic creative music awards. Gerald's work was played by the Columbia Concert Orchestra over CBS and was published by the Ludwig Music Publishing Company, truly remarkable honors for so young a composer. Other recognition was given to Edward Seferian, an outstanding violin student, who won a two hundred dollar scholarship given by the Cleveland Federation of Musicians. In later years, he became the conductor of the Tacoma Symphony Orchestra.

Nineteen hundred forty-nine was memorable as the year of Almeda Adams's death at the age of eighty-four; she was buried in Lake View Cemetery. Her passing was a great loss to the Settlement as well as to the community, but she had had a most productive life — as long as she had been able, she had worked for the welfare of the School. As the years went by after her death, her tremendous contributions were appreciated more and more. The Cleveland Music School Settlement is a shining example of how the zeal of one person can bring untold benefits to a community. Besides the Settlement, Miss Adams had founded the Schumann Society in 1918, a choral group for employed girls. For one with her handicap, the life and accomplishments of Almeda Adams are almost incredible. Living alone and doing all her own cooking and housework almost to the end of her life, she went about with no companion and no seeing-eye dog, and even traveled to Europe alone. She was, of course, a singer who might, under different circumstances, have had a concert career. As an outstanding teacher of voice, she maintained a studio for private pupils and also taught at the Settlement where she headed the voice department for a number of years. She was a pianist, a teacher of piano, and a composer as well. Her *Twilight* for women's voices was published by R. Soehla, and there were many unpublished pieces, including songs (words and music by Miss Adams), which were given in a recital at the Baptist Church of the Master in April 1947. The songs were sung by Miss Adams's last pupil, Dorothy Bergold (now Mrs. Charles Robertson). An operetta, *A Modern Cinderella,* already noted, was another original work.

Almeda Adams was also a writer. She contributed a number of short stories to magazines and wrote a book, *Seeing Europe Through Sightless Eyes,* which brought her world attention. The genesis of the book had come about through the typical concern of Miss Adams for her pupils. She had recognized the golden voice of a young student, Esther Cadkin, and wanted the girl to study in New York. From a music patron, whom Almeda Adams has apprised of Esther's potential as a vocal artist and her need to go to New York to develop this talent further, the girl received the necessary funds. When Esther had finished her instruction in New York, Miss Adams thought it would be of benefit for her to go to Europe and appealed again to the same benefactress. This woman, who remains anonymous and who must have had great admiration for Almeda Adams, once more agreed to finance Esther's study, provided that the teacher accompany her pupil as a chaperon. In this way, Miss Adams made her first tour of Europe, and the book was an account of that journey.

It was later that she returned to Europe alone. One writer, Regina V. Kurlander, in an article in the *Cleveland Plain Dealer* (March 12, 1930), said that Miss Adams continued her lessons in foreign languages and could speak French, German, and Italian fluently. Last, if not least, Almeda Adams was widely known as a lecturer nationally and internationally, and an article appeared about her in the *Reader's Digest* of June 1947. Entitled, "Almeda Adams and Her Seeing Mind," it was written by Thomas M. Johnson and was condensed from the *Christian Herald*. Miss Adams had told Mr. Johnson that we all need seeing minds. "He who lacks the seeing mind is more truly blind than he through whose eyes no light shines," she said. Truly, this woman of tireless energy, determination to overcome misfortune, devotion to teaching, and the power to influence and involve people, was uniquely suited to be founder of such an institution as The Cleveland Music School Settlement.

Because the School was so well-organized, the routine teaching, faculty recitals, and extension work went along quietly throughout 1950, 1951, and 1952. However, a few high points stand out. Since there were no cataclysmic problems stemming from a depression or a war, the trustees and staff could carry out improvements to the building and launch new and imaginative programs. The year 1951 started out with a flourish when the new Kulas Library was opened in January. The occasion was celebrated by a reception honoring Mrs. Elroy J. Kulas, a devoted trustee, and her husband, a leading industrialist. It was their generosity which had made the library possible. The new facility, installed in the old coach house, had shelves of blond oak as well as attractive furniture, and it was equipped with new record players and display cabinets. About a hundred invited guests active in the musical life of the city were received by Mr. and Mrs. Edward W. Garfield and Mr. and Mrs. Kulas. A musical program, in keeping with the traditions and ideals of the School, was given by Josef Gingold and Leonard Shure, while a beautiful reception added to the evening's festivities.

After the death of Mr. Kulas, a faculty recital was given in his memory by Mr. Shure in May 1952. Shortly thereafter, Mrs. Kulas continued to act as a "fairy godmother" to the School by helping in another important house improvement. The Lecture-Recital Club added a matching sum to that of Mrs. Kulas to make this change possible, namely, the enlargement of the recital hall. A partition between the old one and what had been the dining room of the home was removed, and the seating capacity was increased by this alteration from ninety to two hundred and fifty. A platform and new lighting were added, and the new commodious recital hall was redecorated. October 20, 1952 was the day selected for the opening, and the dedicatory concert was performed by distinguished faculty who were also Cleveland Orchestra members: Josef Gingold, Ernest Kardos, Hyman Schandler, Tom Brennand, and Robert Ripley, as well as Leonard Shure and Maurice Goldman. The latter sang compositions by Arthur Shepherd and a new song composed especially for the occasion by Howard Whittaker.

At the end of 1951, a series of concerts featuring American composers was initiated. Inspired by the Bach concerts, which had been presented in 1949 and 1950 and had been so successful and instructive, this new series had the following *raison d'etre* as explained by Howard Whittaker:

> The programs have been chosen to give the Cleveland public as inclusive a picture of American composition — both in point of time as well as place — as it is possible for a series of this size. These performances, we feel, are in answer to a great interest on the part of Cleveland musicians and music lovers to hear works by native composers.

The programs, which extended into 1952, encompassed songs, chamber music, works by some women composers and by Roy Harris, among others. Held in the auditorium of The Cleveland Museum of Art in cooperation with that institution, the first recital in the series, entitled "The Music of Roy Harris," was by far the most noteworthy of the group. Mr. Harris, the eminent, if controversial, American composer, and his wife came to Cleveland for the event and were warmly welcomed by the musical community. Johanna Harris, a skilled pianist, along with Josef Gingold and the faculty string quartet performed, and Mr. Harris spoke briefly during the intermission on "The American Composer." Regarded as "Mr. American Music," Mr. Harris had been characterized by Serge Koussevitsky, renowned conductor of the Boston Symphony Orchestra, as one who expressed with genius American life, its vitality, greatness, and strength. His personality, as well as his music, was challenging, and as one critic, Herbert Elwell (*Cleveland Plain Dealer,* December 15, 1951) wrote: "An adequate appraisal of this complex and profound musical personality can hardly be attempted in a few paragraphs. A 300-page book might be more adequate." The audience was enthusiastic, and guests invited to the Settlement for a reception after the concert had the added pleasure of meeting the composer and his wife. The evening was a stimulating occasion, and the fact that a composer of such stature had participated in this particular series of concerts brought favorable publicity to the School, both locally and nationally.

Mention should be made of several lesser matters that occurred during 1950, 1951, and 1952. The Almeda Adams Club, originally the Parent-Adult Organization, which had been helpful in providing scholarships and serving as a liasion between the School and the parents, had finally disbanded by 1950. In 1951, it was re-activated as the PTA Club, and a number of successful meetings were held which included a series of lectures by an advisory trustee, Miss Barbara Penyak, a librarian in the music division of the Cleveland Public Library. In January of 1952, the Settlement was visited by a musician of international repute, Swiss conductor Ernest Ansermet, who was appearing with The Cleveland Orchestra. An Orchestra member on the faculty brought him to the School, and upon entering the courtyard, the maestro exclaimed, "It's England!"

In February the School, always interested in new ventures, cooperated with the Cleveland public schools and The Cleveland Museum of Art in a program which was the first of its kind to be presented by the Settlement. Arranged to illustrate the varying arts of the Italian Rennaissance, the string ensemble of the School played music of Palestrina and Gabrieli. The purpose of the program was to demonstrate that all the arts are interrelated and to reveal the essential characteristics of a great period of artistic expression.

Howard Whittaker pointed out that

> the program will attempt to show that there can be
> a broadening of the aesthetic experience through
> contact with many forms of art in a given period,
> and an understanding of the forces which molded
> the genius of great artists, whether in music,
> painting, sculpture, architecture, or poetry.

The sliding scale of fees which had been established in 1932 was modified in 1952 to allow for students who wished to pay the full professional fee. Up until that time, the Settlement had accepted only those students in need of financial help. The modification of the policy had come about after a dramatic incident. A father of substantial means persisted in enrolling his daughter at full fee until he finally won, his contention being that the faculty was superior, and that he wanted his daughter to have the experience of associating with young people of different backgrounds.

The death of Winifred Fryer, a trustee, must be noted, since the board minutes of October 1952 speak of her passing as "an irreparable loss." Mrs. Fryer was a member of the executive committee as early as 1924 and had served as treasurer for many years; at her death, she was both vice president and treasurer. In the resolution passed by the board, the following tribute was given:

> In the dark days when the existence and life of
> our School were threatened, she was a tower of
> strength. In times of stress, when decisions were
> often difficult, her wise counsel usually pointed the
> way out of difficulties. When too much seriousness
> or worry overbalanced deliberatons of committees
> or groups, she was always ready with a story to ease
> the situation. It was her aim always to keep before
> our board the purposes for which our School was
> founded, and her far-seeing point of view frequently
> pointed the way to expanding our facilities to
> further those same ideals.

Mrs. Fryer was part of a musical family, several of whose members had ties to the Settlement. Her brother-in-law, Nathan Fryer, at one time head of the piano department, had left a bequest to the School to create a memorial fund in his name. Years later, Mrs. Fryer's nephew, Richard Lurie, a widely known guitarist and teacher, arranged several benefits for the Settlement and its affiliate, Rainey

Institute, whose board of managers he served as chairman.

It has already been recorded that in 1931 the School had abandoned the city-wide caroling program, but when the move was made to Magnolia Drive in 1938, Christmas caroling was resumed as part of the Christmas celebration. The children sang on the terrace of the Settlement, and neighbors were invited to participate; it was a custom followed year after year. On occasions when the weather was inclement, the "Sing" was held indoors. In 1952, when the weather prevented the outdoor caroling, the children's chorus took part instead in the holiday community fund program which was broadcast and shown on television. It was splendid public relations for the Settlement, and much favorable comment was received because of the media exposure.

As 1952 drew to a close, the School was about to enter into the decade which would end with its fiftieth anniversary.

5. The Fifth Decade and the Golden Anniversary

BY 1953, ONE MIGHT SAY that The Cleveland Music School Settlement had reached full maturity. Though now a music school with all the facilites of a private conservatory, it had adhered to its original purpose by continuing to provide services in accordance with the students' ability to pay — it required only that they have a genuine interest in music and be willing to study seriously. Through the extension program, it had helped neighborhood settlement houses with music instruction and was always eager to blaze new trails. One might conclude, too, that the School was something of a concert bureau in offering the many recitals without charge to all who cared to journey to it.

By the 1950s times were more prosperous and this meant rising enrollment which in turn brought in more fees; consequently, more scholarship students could be accommodated. The big problem created by this situation was lack of adequate space to take care of all these students; larger quarters became an urgent need. In March of 1954, a house next to the Settlement was offered for sale, and very soon thereafter the Sherman house adjacent on the other side, formerly the Charles S. Brooks home, was also available. After careful study, the trustees decided in October 1954, that the Brooks house was the one to buy. It was of brick and could be converted to make eleven studios and six lavatories; there was a small theatre in the back yard; and the house and main building could easily be connected.

The next step was to raise funds for the purchase price of twenty-two thousand dollars, and, again, history repeated itself. A friend provided the money, leaving the trustees only the task of raising a sum to put the house in working order for lessons. The good friend in this case was Mrs. Elroy J. Kulas, and the newly acquired facility was named in her honor. The arrangements of the purchase had been worked out with the valuable help of realtor Charles L. Smythe, assistant treasurer of the board. A number of anonymous donors contributed funds for conditioning the house, and other money came from The Cleveland Foundation and the Rotary Clubs of Cleveland. The plan for the use of the Kulas House, which was to include not only regular instruction, but a new type of musical education, was set forth by Howard Whittaker. He said:

> We are particularly pleased to announce a new children's music workshop, especially designed to meet the needs of the pre-school child, four and five years of age. This program is planned as a kind of musical nursery school, which will include rhythm band, singing, musical games, and listening to develop the child's musical instincts as well as appreciation for music. In combining the two fields, music and nursery school, we have approached the beginning of a new phase of musical training for the pre-school child.

The dedication of the new facility in February 1955 was a sparkling event, and the concert in the recital hall was followed by a reception in the Kulas House. The concert itself, as one critic, Rena C. Holtkamp, reported (*Cleveland Plain Dealer,* February 26, 1955), was a brilliant one. She wrote:

> The program opened with the rich vitality of a new *Piano Sonata in A* composed by Director Whittaker for this important occasion in the life of the Settlement and dedicated with appreciation to Mrs. Kulas.
>
> Graceful Tung Kwong Kwong, Chinese concert pianist, gave the sonata its first performance. . . .
> A group of four songs composed by Herbert Elwell, the *Cleveland Plain Dealer* music critic, was presented in a stimulating spirit of songfulness by Maurice Goldman, baritone. . . .
>
> Three members of the Settlement faculty, Leonard Shure, piano, Josef Gingold, violin, and Robert Ripley, cello, presented Beethoven's *Trio in E flat, Op. 1, No. 1* in delightful intimate style as the concluding event of the program.

The dedication was attended by Mrs. Kulas and other friends who had contributed to the project; delegates of the National Guild of Community Music Schools who were in town for their annual conference; and members of the board of trustees, whose president,

Edward W. Garfield, and his wife, headed the welcoming committee. Thus, another milestone had been reached in the progress of the Settlement.

One other physical improvement was accomplished by registration time in the fall of 1955. Increased office space had been needed, and Alexander C. Robinson, III, a trustee and an architect, had submitted plans for remodeling the side porch. It was transformed into a new administration wing consisting of two offices to accommodate the registrar and office manager, respectively, and an outer room for the receptionist, clerical help, and bookkeepers.

Besides its gift for the reconditioning of the Kulas House, The Cleveland Foundation had been generous to the School in other instances. In 1953, for example, it had granted five thousand dollars to aid in the extension of the School's programs into more settlements. The decision to make the grant was the result of many discussions by Foundation representatives with other settlement directors who had requested the School's service. At the outset of these discussions, a trustee, Mrs. Thomas Munro, who also represented the board of The Cleveland Federation of Settlements, had recommended that The Cleveland Music School Settlement provide musical services to all of the ten neighborhood settlements. The Cleveland Foundation planned to review the first year's work in June of 1954, and if it was found to be satisfactory, funding for the project would continue for two more years, making the grand total of fifteen thousand dollars. Richard Kauffman of the St. Louis Institute of Music, who had been chosen in 1953 to head this extension program, was performing his duties in an exemplary fashion, and it is of interest to give a review of what he accomplished in his early years.

Mr. Kauffman's first task had been to procure a staff to carry out this new program. Through consultation with Ward Lewis, acting director of The Cleveland Institute of Music, and Marie Martin, head of its children's theory program, Mr. Kauffman obtained as the first teachers for the Settlement's extension program: Joseph C. Robinson, (later, in 1972, staff member of the Cleveland board of education's supplementary educational center), and Mary Santoli (Mrs. Mike DeLuca). The program was designed to furnish good music in each neighborhood, to provide constructive recreation, and to acquaint the participating centers with similar programs in other parts of the city.

To realize these goals, various new methods were adopted. An intrumental demonstration program, geared to pre-school children's interests, was begun through the request of Mimi Shifron, director of the Jewish Day Nursery. Pianist Patricia Cox developed this program, and she worked with Robert Fields, clarinetist. Of importance also were the annual inter-settlement music festivals held at WHK Studio One, in which all the agencies of the neighborhood centers and the Jewish Community Center participated. In fact, the latter's Arlington, Shaker Lee, and Heights branches requested and paid for the services of the extension program from 1953 until its own facility was built on Mayfield Road in 1960. Also popular were exchange programs within the neighborhood centers. Audiences at the neighborhood center programs had the opportunity to hear some of the city's finest musicians; members of The Cleveland Orchestra, who were on the faculty of the Settlement, performed for them. One such program in the spring of 1954 was given by James Barrett, violin; Tom Brennand, viola, and Robert Ripley, cello. Other faculty artists appeared in recital at the neighborhood centers, and gifted students as well were given an opportunity to participate.

In order to provide news to these centers and the Jewish Community Center participating in the extension program, a monthly newspaper, *The Music Makers,* was started. One of its issues included an editorial by the well-known, former *Cleveland Press* chief editorial writer, Richard D. Peters; he had served as president of the National Federation of Settlements and Neighborhood Centers at the time that he was the editor, later in his career, of the *World Telegram and Sun* in New York City. Another publication that was distributed was a songbook, *Cleveland Sings,* in which all the songs had been selected by the neighborhood centers' staffs and program participants.

In the spring of 1954, twenty-five music clubs from twelve settlements with a total of two hundred and sixty-three participants took part in the first city-wide music festival; more than a thousand were in the audience. At Christmas time in 1954, all the neighborhood centers collaborated in programs entitled "A Children's Christmas Celebration" at the Cleveland Public Library; these were under the auspices of the Library's fine arts department. Included in the proceedings were such emcees as Dr. Rudolph Ringwall, associate conductor of The Cleveland Orchestra, Howard Whittaker, and others. In addition, an all-city original composition contest was held; judges included Herbert Elwell, Starling Cumberworth, Bain Murray, and Mr. Whittaker, all from the Settlement. These endeavors were important, not only because they were furthering the purposes of the extension program, but also because they were making the community more aware of the Settlement, especially in the less affluent neighborhoods.

So successful were the varied activities in the extension program, that in October 1954 a young man from Germany, Johannes Klotz, a guest in this country through the courtesy of the National Social Welfare Assembly and the United States state department, spent three months with Mr. Kauffman observing the School's extension work in the neighborhood centers. Mr. Klotz was followed in succeeding years by other visitors: Mrs. Takako Ogishima from Japan; Klaus Fiedler from Germany, and Tino Kerdijk from Indonesia.

Beginning in 1954, the extension program originated inter-settlement club, class, and rehearsal parties. All these activities were designed to bring people from different parts of the city closer together through music. Another innovative project of the extension program was made possible through the efforts of a trustee, Mrs. T. Wingate Todd. This was an arrangement whereby the young people affiliated with the neighborhood centers, together with their families, could attend the concerts of the Cleveland Philharmonic Orchestra. Since the extension program stressed family participation, as many as eight hundred from the centers attended a concert at one time.

In 1956, the extension program introduced opera, the first one being Pergolesi's *The Maid as Mistress,* with Beverly Dame, soprano; John Dietz, baritone; Richard Kauffman, mute part, and Rosa Lobe, piano. In later years, other operas were presented, which featured vocalists Joseph C. Robinson, Dorothy DeVaughn, Evelyn Morgan, George Kleinfeld, Jane Hitchcock, and Miss Dame, with pianists Patricia Cox and Mrs. Lobe, all very fine artists who were willing to share their talents with the audiences at the neighborhood centers.

The grant which The Cleveland Foundation had made to the extension program in 1953, with renewal for three years contingent upon the first year's success, had been unequivocally extended for the full period. At the end of that time, the president of the Settlement's board, in writing to thank the Foundation, pointed out that the National Federation of Settlements had shown great interest in this program, and that it had sent a staff member to Cleveland to study the work that was being done within the inner city and other low income areas. This was a fitting tribute to Richard Kauffman's work with the extension program.

Returning to the activities of the main school in 1953, one finds there was renewed interest in vocal instruction, and Maurice Goldman was now head of the voice department. A spring festival included a production called "Rumpelstilskin" by the junior chorus and Benjamin Britten's *The Rape of Lucretia* under the direction of Mr. Goldman. The next year the Settlement cooperated with The Junior League of Cleveland, Inc. in presenting deFalla's *Master Peter's Puppet Show.* A program of contemporary vocal and operatic repertoire was also given, and every work was a premiere for Cleveland. Included were *Abraham's Sacrifice* by Britten; *Cantata* by Igor Stravinsky based on anonymous fifteenth and sixteenth century English lyrics, and *Bluebeard's Castle,* a one-act opera by Bela Bartok. This program was introduced by Maurice Goldman, who discussed the music to be heard and the plans he had for other events arranged to interest audiences in twentieth century music. Herbert Elwell, music critic of the *Cleveland Plain Dealer,* pronounced the concert "an example of how stimulating an evening of modern music can be."

One of the recitals in 1954 was given by Jaime Laredo, a brilliant pupil of Josef Gingold. This event is notable in retrospect since Mr. Laredo was to achieve international fame and become the most celebrated pupil the School had so far produced. Another event worthy of note in 1954 was not a musical recital, but a lecture by Arthur Loesser, the distinguished Cleveland pianist, teacher, critic, and author, who talked about his newly published book, *Men, Women and Pianos;* this book sold so well that it was later produced in paperback form.

An important all-Stravinsky program took place in December of 1955. Mr. Stravinsky, who was in town for Cleveland Orchestra concerts, was invited, but, unfortunately, he was not able to attend. The music aroused spirited comment, and the critics in their reviews the next day differed in their opinions. Arthur Loesser disliked much of it, while Herbert Elwell called the performance "a fascinatingly adventurous musical evening." Such controversy served to liven the cultural life of the city.

The School was ever mindful of maintaining its standards, and for this reason, in January of 1956, Director Whittaker recommended to the trustees that there be a policy of evaluating students. He thought that those who did not take their work seriously should be discontinued. There was a large enough waiting list of young people eager to work and avail themselves of an opportunity for a musical education, and the trustees approved this policy to improve the quality of the students enrolled.

As the year unfolded, the Welfare Federation requested that studies be made of all its agencies. In years past there had been the survey by Mr. and Mrs. Ramsey. This time, Miss Grace Spofford was chosen to study the instruction and to appraise the School's overall operation. Especially well qualified, she had begun at the Henry Street Settlement in New York City as director of its music school and vice president of the National Guild of Community Music Schools. It is interesting to note that Dr. Robert Egan, former student and teacher at The Cleveland Music School Settlement, succeeded Miss Spofford in her position at the Henry Street Settlement; he later became dean of music at Duquesne University in Pittsburgh.

Miss Spofford's report, read to the trustees at their annual meeting in May of 1956, was highly commendatory. She stated the following:

> The teachers of the School are of uncommon excellence, musically and academically, many of them holding advanced degrees and averaging five years experience in Settlement teaching. In addition they posses human qualities of personal interest in their students.
>
> I observed the library program, several theory classes, the modern dance classes, and the nursery school. All of these are excellent, the library program being unique in teaching young people to listen under controlled conditions.

She examined the budget, the School curriculum, the special activities, the extension program, and the physical plant. Her conclusion was:

> The Cleveland Music School Settlement is housed in the best physical plant of any community music school. Its board, administration, staff, and faculty show imagination and accomplishment of the highest order. Its students have taken their places in the community.

Miss Spofford made some suggestions for strengthening certain departments and proposed some additions to the curriculum. She recommended increases in salary for the teachers, augmentation of funds for scholarship, the establishment of an endowment fund, as well as a west side branch. (The suggestion for a new branch was to be carried out before too long.) Were these recommendations to be implemented, she predicted, "the pattern developed here would be a model for other cities." It should be pointed out that such a positive report reflected to a large extent the contributions made by many trustees who took care of countless details in the operation of the School. For example, in the 1940s and 1950s Frank James gave the Settlement invaluable assistance in procuring adequate insurance for buildings, contents, and liability. While this work did not improve the teaching or programs of the Settlement, it did ensure that the School could continue to function even if disasters such as fire or burglary should occur. When there was a fire and some burglary, the importance of this voluntary work became strikingly apparent.

At the beginning of 1956, Edward W. Garfield told the board that by June he would complete twenty-five years as president, and though he would always be concerned with the School's welfare, he would like to be relieved of the major responsibility. The trustees were well aware of the fact that during his presidency, the School had grown from a relatively small student body to an enrollment of approximately one thousand students in the main school, five hundred in the extension program, and that it had achieved a prominent position among music school settlements in the nation. The board wanted to show its appreciation for Mr. Garfield's long and dedicated service in some tangible way, and an evening in May 1956 was selected to honor him and Mrs. Garfield.

The festivities began with a most unusual musical program arranged by Howard Whittaker. One of the features was a performance by Carol Sindell, the seven-year-old precocious violin pupil of Josef Gingold. (At the end of the year, she played the first two movements of a Mozart concerto with the Suburban Symphony conducted by Robert C. Weiskopf, later to become an advisory trustee.) Another part of the program for the Garfields demonstrated how the School met the needs of young and old; it was a performance by a family ensemble composed of Mrs. Carol Otto, pianist, and her three daughters, all of whom were studying at the Settlement — flute, violin, and cello being their instruments. Maurice Goldman, faculty member, sang a song composed by Mr. Whittaker and dedicated to Mr. Garfield. Finally, as evidence of the superior musical performances that the School offered to the Cleveland public, there were selections played by Josef Gingold, faculty member and concertmaster of The Cleveland Orchestra. A reception honoring the Garfields followed. At the time of his retirement, Mr. Garfield, grandson of the twentieth president of the United States, had served the School as president of the board for more than half of its existence.

The next president elected in May 1956 was Edward F. Meyers, who had been serving as treasurer since 1952. Mrs. Elroy J. Kulas, vice-president, was the logical successor to Mr. Garfield. She preferred, however, not to serve and suggested Mr. Meyers for the office. The first meeting of the board under his leadership was held in September at the home of Mrs. Kulas. Wives and husbands of trustees were invited to meet Mr. Meyers and to hear about plans for the remainder of 1956. It was announced that Mrs. Kulas had demonstrated her generosity again by contributing money for the breezeway to be built between the Kulas House and the main building. Howard Whittaker could not be present at the meeting; he was in Toronto on invitation of its University Settlement School to confer with the trustees and Canadian government officials on the expansion of that school. From there, he was to go on to St. Louis to assist its community fund in a survey of music school activities. These trips pointed up the high regard in which the Cleveland director was held, an esteem which reflected credit on the School.

The faculty recitals in 1956 continued to focus on contemporary music. In January, Josef Gingold, violinist, and Harold Heiberg, pianist, played works of Ernest Bloch, Marcel Dick, and Herbert Elwell; in March, Maurice Goldman presented songs by Samuel Barber, Igor Stravinsky, Modest Moussorgsky, and Cleveland's Elwell, Whittaker, Robert Fields, and Goldman himself. A special concert in March honored Ernest Bloch, the first director of The Cleveland Institute of Music, with a performance of his *String Quartet, No. 3,* and excerpts from his opera, *Macbeth.* In December, there was a concert of contemporary vocal music. Herbert Elwell who had been on the faculty as teacher of composition since 1954, wrote in his review (*Cleveland Plain Dealer,* December 18, 1956): "Goldman must be complimented not only for skillful direction but for the spirit of inquiry and adventure which led to the assembly of so much new music of high quality."

Absent from these faculty recitals was Leonard Shure, to whom, in March 1956, the trustees had granted a leave of absence for one year to fulfill concert and recording engagements. During his leave Mr. Shure made the decision to live in New York, thus severing his connection with the School and necessitating a search for a new head of the piano department.

In January of 1957, Mrs. Kulas helped to carry out one of the recommendations in Miss Grace Spofford's report by giving the School three thousand dollars as the nucleus for a Settlement endowment fund; in addition, she offered to match other gifts, within reason, and some months later added a larger sum to the fund. In September 1957 everyone connected with the School was to be greatly saddened by the death of this most benevolent friend. In her obituary it was mentioned how much she had done, not only for The Cleveland Music School Settlement (Mr. Whittaker later reported that within the previous fifteen years she and her husband had contributed one hundred and twenty-five thousand dollars), but also for music in general throughout the Cleveland area. The Settlement had been graced by her presence, and administrators, faculty, and students had benefited from her wise counsel.

When the will of Mrs. Kulas became known, it was patent that her thoughtfulness of the Settlement had been extended beyond her life; she had provided for an annual grant from the Kulas Foundation and, in addition, left a handsome sum outright. She had stipulated that three quarters of the annual grant be used for scholarships; the balance was to assist in the purchase of musical instruments for worthy and needy pupils and also to provide for personal expenses of the director or his assistants in furthering the interests of the School.

In May 1957 the search for a new head of the piano department was ended by the appointment of Theodore Lettvin. A distinguished young master pianist, he was a product of the Curtis Institute of Music where he had studied with Rudolf Serkin. Mr. Lettvin had already won many honors and, in accordance with the wish of the trustees, was to give full time to the position. He took up his duties in September and gave his first faculty recital the next month. As a prologue to this concert, the slow movement from Howard Whittaker's *Piano Sonata in A* was played as a tribute to Mrs. Kulas.

In 1957, Mr. Whittaker, having been director for almost ten years, asked for a six-month sabbatical to devote more time to his work as a composer. The trustees agreed that this leave should be granted, and beginning in November, Richard Kauffman, head of the extension program, took over the director's duties. Perhaps the most exciting thing that had occurred so far at the Settlement, an event with international repercussions, was the visit of representatives from the Voice of America. At the time, this global radio network of the United States Information Agency (USIA) broadcasted by shortwave in thirty-six languages around the clock and around the world to audiences numbering in the millions. The representatives visited shortly before Mr. Whittaker left on his sabbatical.

The Voice had for some time been seeking a school where teachers spoke foreign languages, and Mrs. Edward W. Hollis, chairman of the board's publicity committee, had somehow been apprised of this desire. The final result was that one morning a bus rolled up to the School discharging thirty-five people who came for interviews with students and teachers. Engaged by the Voice of America, they were from all over the world and on occasion acted as interpreters for the state department. Forty-three interviews in many foreign languages took place. One of the most touching was with a six-year-old boy who studied violin and who had just escaped with his family from Hungary. A Cleveland newspaper article appeared after this visit and bears quoting:

> Refugees of all ages, no matter what their native tongue, gravitate to The Cleveland Music School Settlement, and the universal language of music helps them adjust to their new life. Instruments which they studied but left behind as they fled are loaned to them. They are placed with a teacher who speaks their language. . . . In the past ten years, over three hundred students from almost every country in the world have studied at the Music Settlement, and some have made music their career.

Some time later, the Voice of America beamed out the taped interviews in a series of programs to many countries of Europe. In due course, letters began to arrive at the School, and it was thrilling both to read the comments of these strangers who had so enjoyed the programs and to learn that the School's reputation had become so widespread.

Since Mr. Meyers wished to relinquish the duties of the presidency after two years, Alexander C. Robinson, III was elected to that office at the annual meeting in May 1958. Richard Kauffman reported on his six months as acting director and said that the rapport among faculty, students, and parents was excellent. As examples he cited — a student activities bulletin board had been added in the main lounge; a "new look" had been taken at student recitals, which resulted in all-girls and all-boys concerts as well as a family ensemble recital, the latter having eighteen groups in which two or more members of the same family participated; one parent-teachers' meeting had been arranged, and a music theory week had been proclaimed, with special invitations to parents and faculty from other departments to attend theory classes; there had been three faculty-staff parties, and a trustee-faculty party had been jointly planned; finally, faculty members representing various departments had been presented at the trustees' meetings. Mr. Kauffman added that through the interest of faculty and parents, several new groups had been started: a rhythm and crafts class for five-year-olds, the purpose of which was to bridge the gap between nursery school and the beginning of music theory; a trombone quartet, and a school orchestra which Miss Grace Spofford had recommended.

Mr. Kauffman went on to say that, in accordance with the School's policy of searching out new ways for providing assistance, two meetings had been scheduled at the Cleveland board of education to discuss with the elementary, junior, and senior high instrumental instructors the teaching needs of the community and to discern what the Settlement might do to help. He mentioned that physical improvements to the School buildings encompassed the installation of record listening booths in the library, new railings on the entrance porch, and landscaping for the front of the house.

In May when Mr. Whittaker returned from his sabbatical, he reported to the trustees about the compositions he had written during his stay in Guadalajara, Mexico. In an article concerning the director's sojourn, Herbert Elwell wrote that Mr. Whittaker had benefited not only from the absence of administrative responsibilities but also from an environment conducive to creativity. He had found in Mexico an uncommon respect for those with artistic ability. When Mr. Whittaker had become known there as a composer, his newly made friends began treating him with a deference not usually accorded to *norteamericanos*.

The establishment of the West Side Branch, another of Miss Spofford's recommendations, was realized in 1958. Major factors in bringing this about had been discussions with west side instrumental instructors from the Cleveland board of education and a grant from The Cleveland Foundation. Within a short time one hundred and fifty students were enrolled in the Saturday program. Violinist Jeanette Drinkall Meyer, who had studied with Josef Gingold, was the first director. She was very effective in launching the branch and was succeeded by Paul Neal, tenor and composer, several years later.

Theodore Lettvin, head of the piano department, brought renown to the School in 1958. He was chosen by the cultural committee of the state department to be one of five pianists to play at the American Pavilion of the Brussels World's Fair. He also gave concerts in other European cities which included Mr. Whittaker's sonata. Upon Mr. Lettvin's return, the mayor and city council of Cleveland prepared a resolution congratulating him and expressing their appreciation for his having brought honor and pride to all residents of the community. In a faculty recital with Josef Gingold, in December, Mr. Lettvin made his first appearance of the season since his successful concert tour abroad. Not only was the recital a particularly outstanding one, but the evening was made festive by Mr. and Mrs. Robinson's reception honoring the two artists after the concert. Among the guests were the distinguished visiting conductor of The Cleveland Orchestra, Stanislaw Skrowaczewski, and his wife, both from Poland.

At the end of 1958, the Kulas Foundation continued its generosity to the School by granting twelve thousand dollars for the purchase of nineteen new upright pianos. This was fortunate because the second term of the 1958-59 year saw an increase of two hundred and eleven in enrollment; the number of students at the main school was now well over one thousand, while six hundred studied in the extension program. In March after a unit cost study had been made by the finance committee of the board, it was approved by the trustees to raise the lesson fees by fifty cents in all but two departments in order to keep the full fees in line with those charged elsewhere.

An article in the *Cleveland Plain Dealer* (March 10, 1959) demonstrated how chance could play a part in helping the School. In it was recounted that when the newspaper had printed the Give-a-Christmas stories, one had been a particular plea for a violin for a talented little girl whose mother could not afford to buy the instrument. Immediately, the Give-a-Christmas headquarters had been deluged with more than forty offers. The child, whose plight had been told, received her violin, but the newspaper wondered what to do about the others. It was then, the article reported, that The Cleveland Music School Settlement came to the rescue. "This is our job," a spokesman for the school told the reporter. "We not only lend instruments to students but we see that lessons are arranged on a sliding scale of fees. In cases of extreme need, full scholarships for talented students are to be had." As a result, the newspaper reported that the School had already collected twenty-six violins and more were being picked up daily. After Josef Gingold, head of the violin department, had looked over one heap of instruments, he spotted a twin violin case containing two good violins. "That's a rare case — made by Hill of London, probably worth several hundred dollars," he observed. Howard Whittaker, who was also quoted in this article, said that the School needed wind and brass instruments as well as pianos. This plea also brought results.

As in the previous academic year, the School announced March 30th through April 4th as music theory and library week. Parents were invited to attend classes in preparatory group music; theory and harmony; solfege; form and analysis, and classes in music literature and music history. "Our teachers," the announcement advised, "will demonstrate many important aspects of our Theory Program and talk with parents about their children's progress."

At this time Robert Fields, the assistant director, left the School to become the director of the Community Music School of Buffalo (later he became director of the Community Music Center in San Francisco). Charles Campbell replaced Mr. Fields at the School as assistant to Howard Whittaker.

In May of 1959, the School joined with other area musical organizations in launching a "May Show" of music, dubbed the Cleveland May Festival of Contemporary Music. In the foreword of the program, Walter Blodgett, Settlement advisory trustee and curator of musical arts at The Cleveland Museum of Art, wrote:

> For several years many people have felt that Cleveland should have a series of concerts to parallel in music what is done in the field of visual arts by the famous May Show of The Cleveland Museum of Art. The forty-first annual opening today of this notable event now has a musical

counterpart.

In 1950 the Museum's department of musical arts attempted a series of May programs of contemporary music. This modest beginning was successful, but limitations of funds and space prohibited a truly adequate project. Several months ago invitations were sent to musical insitutions of the University Circle area to collaborate on a plan which would permit a wide and varied survey of contemporary music. Oberlin Conservatory of Music was invited also because for many years it has produced a similar festival. All accepted with great enthusiasm. . . .

The participating institutions (in addition to The Cleveland Music School Settlement) are: The Cleveland Orchestra, George Szell, music director, Robert Shaw, associate director, and A. Beverly Barksdale, manager; The Cleveland Institute of Music, Ward Davenny, director; Oberlin Conservatory of Music, David Robertson, dean; Western Reserve University, John S. Millis, president, Edward G. Evans, department of music, and Barclay S. Leathem, department of drama; The Cleveland Museum of Art, Sherman E. Lee, director, and Walter Blodgett, curator of musical arts. The University Circle Development Foundation, through its president, Neil J. Carothers, has given great and generous assistance. . . .

It was the policy of the planning committee to draw upon the wide world of music, to gather together works of contemporary spirit and excellence. Therefore, the repertory includes music by composers of international repute as well as by esteemed composers of the environs of Cleveland. Works were admitted on the basis of quality, not because they were merely new. A number of Cleveland first performances will occur during the festival. . . .

The concerts were held in The Cleveland Museum of Art with the exception of the orchestra and opera programs. The Settlement's concert included works by Serge Prokofiev, Arthur Shepherd, Howard Whittaker, and Starling Cumberworth, head of the theory department. Herbert Elwell, commenting on this program, wrote:

> Starling Cumberworth's *Sonata for Violin and Piano in G,* played "con amore" by Josef Gingold, violin, and Theodore Lettvin, piano, proved to be one of the most delightful new works heard here for some time. . . .
>
> The folk song element was present also in Howard Whittaker's *Sonata for Cello and Piano in F,* although in a more jubilant and externalized manner. Not less interesting in its way than the preceding sonata, it developed with exhilarating rhythmic contrasts, gave the cello difficult but attractively expressive lines, and left one with an impression of strong vitality and laudable craftsmanship. It was given an extremely effective realization by Ernst Silberstein, cello, and Andrius Kuprevicius, piano.

At the trustees meeting in May 1959, Mr. Robinson spoke of the great need for adding to the generous gifts made in 1957 by Mrs. Elroy J. Kulas; she had wished to encourage the establishment of a Settlement endowment fund, and it was unanimously approved to undertake a drive for this purpose. The Welfare Federation granted special permission for this effort, its only stipulation being that the drive be concluded in one year. When October came, the board was given a sixteen-page brochure that had been produced by Mrs. Edward W. Hollis, chairman of the publicity committee, with substantial help from Howard Skidmore of the Chesapeake and Ohio Railroad (Mr. Skidmore subsequently became a trustee of the Settlement).

Through the years the Settlement produced many outstanding musicians. In 1954, when Jaime Laredo, the promising pupil of Josef Gingold, was thirteen years old, he had, as mentioned before, given a recital at the School. It is doubtful that anyone who heard that concert envisioned the boy as attaining international reputation within five years. Laredo had been helped with scholarships given by the Cleveland Chamber Music Society and the Cleveland Chapter, Society for Strings, Inc., the latter group having presented Laredo in a professional debut in 1956. He had gone from The Cleveland

Music School Settlement to the Curtis Institute of Music, where he studied with the legendary Ivan Galamian. Now in 1959 he had been catapulted into world-wide fame, when he won the Queen Elisabeth International Music Competition in Belgium, the youngest recipient ever to have been awarded the prize. This biennial event alternates between violinists and pianists; thus, violinists may enter once every four years. Musicians up to thirty years of age are eligible, and the competition is one of the most prestigious. Since it was reported throughout the world that Jaime Laredo had studied at The Cleveland Music School Settlement, it is of interest to learn how Jaime, a Bolivian, came to the School.

He had been born in Cochabamba, Bolivia, in 1941 of Inca and Spanish parents. Coming from a family of music lovers, he had shown signs of musical ability when he was very young. His first teacher, Carlo Flamini, advised his parents to take him to the United States to continue his studies. In 1948 he was brought to San Francisco, where he worked with Antonio de Grassi and Frank Houser, who was a member of the San Francisco Orchestra and played during the summers with a string quartet at the music festival in Albuquerque, New Mexico. Josef Gingold was also a member of this quartet, and Mr. Houser talked to him about his talented pupil and eventually persuaded the Settlement's master teacher to accept Jaime as a pupil. So it was that the boy's parents brought him to Cleveland, where, with scholarship help, he continued his studies at the School.

After winning the Queen Elisabeth of Belgium prize, the young virtuoso was invited to appear as soloist with The Cleveland Orchestra under George Szell in October 1959; in a recital debut at Carnegie Hall in New York the same month; with the National Symphony in Washington, D.C. in November, and with the Philadelphia Orchestra under Eugene Ormandy in December. He was awarded the highest honor of Bolivia, El Condor of the Andes Order, and returned there to receive this recognition. Just before his departure, his father telephoned all of those who had helped his son — Howard Whittaker; a trustee, Dr. Lester G. Glick, who was also affiliated with the Cleveland Chapter, Society for Strings; Robert C. Weiskopf of the same Society, and Mr. and Mrs. Gingold. As soloist with The Cleveland Orchestra, Jaime Laredo was the first artist in many years to perform with the Orchestra during the opening week of concerts, this week generally having an orchestral program.

Mr. Laredo called this Severance Hall debut "a magnificient homecoming" which was celebrated appropriately at the Settlement when Mr. and Mrs. Alexander C. Robinson, III entertained with a reception after the initial concert.

In 1959, the wider world of music was being awakened to the existence of the School, not only because of Jaime Laredo's dramatic ascent to fame, but also through the extremely gifted members of the composition department. In South America that summer, the name of The Cleveland Music School Settlement was mentioned widely when a concert series given in Montevideo, Uruguay, included works by many American composers. Three of the works chosen were by Howard Whittaker, Herbert Elwell, and Starling Cumberworth, and their positions with the Settlement were referred to in press releases and biographical notes of the programs.

In November 1959 it became known that Josef Gingold, head of the violin department for thirteen years, beloved teacher who had nurtured the talents of such as Jaime Laredo, Carol Sindell, and many others, was resigning as concertmaster of The Cleveland Orchestra and from the faculty to become a music professor at Indiana University in Bloomington. He gave his last solo performance with the Orchestra in December, but he was to finish out the school year before leaving the city. His pupil, Carol Sindell, appeared with the Orchestra at a Twilight Concert in November; at eleven years of age, she was the youngest soloist ever to appear with The Cleveland Orchestra. (Earlier in the year, Mr. Gingold had brought Mischa Elman, world famed violinist and head of the Curtis Institute of Music, to hear her play at the Settlement.) In fact, this particular season the Settlement had had three members of its faculty, Josef Gingold, Theodore Lettvin, and Andrius Kuprevicius, as well as the student, Carol Sindell, and the former student, Jaime Laredo, as guest soloists with the Orchestra.

Memorable days on the calendar of the Settlement in 1960 were March 31st and April 2nd when The Cleveland Orchestra played a composition by Howard Whittaker in its regular series. This was under the direction of George Szell, and the work chosen was Mr. Whittaker's *Two Murals for Orchestra;* it had been inspired by Orozco's paintings. Two receptions were given for Mr. Whittaker celebrating the occasion — the first one by the board was held at the School after the Thursday evening concert, and the other was given by William G. Lantz, II, a trustee, and his wife at their home in Gates Mills following the Saturday night concert. Among the guests at the latter were Señor Alberto Becerra, Mexican consul, and Señor Estaban Morales, vice-consul, both of Detroit.

Another event of importance, one which exemplified the cooperation of the organizations in the vicinity of the School and their desire to offer programs of benefit and pleasure to the public, was a religious festival sponsored by the Church of the Covenant. The object of the festival, as stated in the program, was "to bring to people a realization of the use of contemporary arts and the impact of them on the present day religious scene." The festival included talks on architecture, ceramic sculpture, enamels, and stained glass as they pertained to churches and church services, as well as an exhibit, "Visual Arts for the Church." Another part of the festival was a production of the opera, *Noye's Fludde*. The music was written by Benjamin Britten, who had become England's most celebrated composer; the text was that of the mediaeval Chester miracle play of the same name. The performance was given in the Church of the Covenant just as the miracle plays were enacted in the cathedrals of old; the Settlement furnished most of the players for the orchestra, which was made up primarily of young people.

For a long time the School had been encouraging the performance of works by contemporary composers, and most of the faculty recitals included at least one, often by a Cleveland composer. Three faculty members, Starling Cumberworth, Bain Murray, and Howard Whittaker, belonged to The Cleveland Composers Guild; it had sponsored several concerts at the School in 1960, at which works by local composers were performed. One program featured music written exclusively for the young musician. Frank Hruby in *The Cleveland Press* wrote: "Cleveland and be justly proud of its core of composers, growing yearly in size and consequence." It is of some interest to know the origins of the Composers Guild, because it was a section of The Fortnightly Musical Club, a major force in the cultural life of the community. The Club had been very supportive of the School, since its doors first opened, by making an annual contribution. The publication, *Fine Arts Magazine, A Weekly Guide* (March 27, 1960), gives a good resume of the Guild's history. To quote from this account:

> The origins of the Composers Guild go back to the 1920s when a small group of Fortnightly Club members met privately to perform and discuss their

own works under the guidance of Charles V. Rychlik, a prominent east side teacher of violin. Over the years this interest was maintained in the Club's manuscript section. Three years ago when Mrs. Carl Corner became chairman of the group, plans to reach a larger audience in the community began to take shape. During that season the efforts of Mrs. Corner, Donald Erb, Robert Fields, now director of the Buffalo Community Music School, and many others resulted in one public concert of original Cleveland works. During the following season of 1958-59, two concerts were presented in the fall and spring. At the beginning of the current season, the manuscript section, officially re-dedicated as the Composers Guild, began an impressive series of public concerts which will soon number eight in all.

Several local composers were becoming interested in Oriental music, and the School scheduled an illustrated lecture on Indonesian music. Through a cultural exchange for the broadening of popular musical instruction, the United States state department had sponsored the visit to America of Tino Kerdijk, director of a private music school in Surabaya, Java. Mr. Kerdijk gave a lecture on the forms of Indonesian music, using recordings of widely varying character. One selection was especially interesting, as the music was played with instruments made entirely of shell. Such music, because of its strangeness and unfamiliarity, was especially intriguing to Western composers and instrumentalists.

The most eloquent and moving concert of this school year was that of Josef Gingold in June 1960. A benefit to establish a scholarship fund in Mr. Gingold's name, it was held in the Severance Chamber Music Hall. He is reputed to have said that no greater honor had ever come to him than the creation of this scholarship fund. Mr. Gingold had been a settlement student in New York when he had first come to the United States, and he knew from personal experience the importance of a scholarship. The program included some remarks by Alexander C. Robinson, III, president, who paid tribute to Mr. Gingold's many years of service to the Settlement. Mr. Gingold responded, "I am proud to have lived to see this day and prouder still to have been on the faculty of the School." More than three thousand dollars was raised by the concert, and additional funds were subscribed later. In the fall Muriel Moebius, a sixth grader at the Broadway school in Maple Heights, was awarded the first Gingold Scholarship.

That Mr. Gingold was held in greatest esteem had been manifest at a benefit concert given in the spring sponsored by the Cleveland Chapter, Society for Strings, for which Jaime Laredo had contributed his services. At this performance, Mr. Gingold, as his former teacher, was the recipient of two citations; both designated April 21 as Josef Gingold Day. One was a proclamation from Governor Michael V. DiSalle and was read by Attorney General Mark McElroy; the other from Mayor Anthony J. Celebrezze was read by the Cleveland law director, Ralph S. Locher. But it was the reviews which followed Mr. Gingold's concert in June that more nearly expressed the feeling of his friends and associates as well as of those who had often been in his audiences. Frank Hruby of *The Cleveland Press* (June 8, 1960) wrote: "The printed programs were blue in the Severance Recital Hall last night and so were, figuratively, a good many of Josef Gingold's friends and admirers." The *Cleveland Plain Dealer* (June 8, 1960) critic Ethel Boros said:

> Officially, the program for Josef Gingold's farewell concert last night listed works by Beethoven, Elwell and Brahms, but the entire program was a love song, an expression of the humane feeling which violinist Gingold has always shown toward his fellow man.

In the fall of 1960, Howard Whittaker informed the trustees with justifiable pride that the six students awarded the certificate of accomplishment in June had received full four-year scholarships to the following conservatories and colleges: Eastman School of Music; Oberlin Conservatory of Music; University of Arizona; Rollins College; and Western Reserve University. This record attests to the high standards of teaching at the Settlement.

The drive for the Settlement endowment fund, which had been undertaken in 1959, was proceeding slowly. Mr. Robinson announced to the board in December of 1960 that eighty-seven hundred dollars had been raised — far less than the desired goal — but it was a beginning. At the same time, the president was happy to report that The Louis D. Beaumont Foundation, The Cleveland Foundation, the Kulas Foundation, and The Leonard C. Hanna,

Jr., Final Fund had approved grants to help the School with scholarships and salaries, until it could accumulate enough endowment to generate more income.

By 1961 the Settlement had gained quite a reputation for its training of staff members who later became directors of other community music schools. Certainly, this was a compliment to Howard Whittaker's leadership. The 1959 appointment of Robert Fields to a Buffalo post has already been mentioned, and in the fall of 1961, Charles Campbell, assistant to the director, became director of the Wilmington Music School in Delaware. He was succeeded at the Settlement by John Shurtleff.

In an overall view of the years, 1961 and 1962, it is evident that the major attention of the trustees, the faculty, and the administrative staff was focused upon the endowment fund drive and the celebration of the golden anniversary. Robert D. Thum was chosen from the board of trustees as chairman of the drive. To bring attention to this fund-raising effort, a luncheon was held in January 1961, at The Halle Bros. Co., a co-sponsor of the event. Van Cliburn, the highly publicized winner of the Tchaikovsky International Piano Competition in Moscow, who had come to Cleveland to play a recital that evening, was to to have been the "star" attraction at the luncheon. He was forced to cancel at the last moment, and Theodore Lettvin, head of the piano department, replaced him and gave a brilliant performance. Muriel Moebius, the Gingold Award recipient, also performed, which demonstrated to guests the quality of students receiving scholarship assistance. Mr. Thum was toastmaster to what turned out to be a very impressive occasion despite Van Cliburn's cancellation.

In May of 1961, President Robinson told the assembled trustees that a sum of twenty thousand dollars had been pledged to the Settlement endowment fund by an anonymous donor, provided that a matching sum be raised by the end of January. It was announced in March of 1962 that the anonymous gift, then known to have offered by Mrs. Dudley S. Blossom, had been over-matched by one thousand seven hundred and thirty-one dollars. The final tally on the endowment drive was given by Mr. Robinson at the annual meeting in May 1962. To quote his words:

> Our endowment fund, while not reaching our
> hoped for goal, has brought the Settlement before
> the community as never before. We raised in

pledges and cash gifts over ninety-eight thousand dollars which, together with the thirty-eight thousand dollars already in the fund before the drive, amounts to one hundred and thirty-six thousand dollars. Many pledges still due over a period of years will swell this figure. We also know of bequests which will come to us and already have received five thousand dollars from the Nathan Fryer estate.

In this effort for the endowment, we owe our thanks to Mrs. Edward W. Hollis and her husband for....sparking the undertaking of the drive and producing the magnificent brochure we had, which tells the story of the Settlement and its needs; and to Robert D. Thum for carrying on the drive with energy and enthusiasm. Our thanks also go to all of you good board members who have worked in contacting donors and have given us your support financially as well, many of you repeating your gifts annually. There have been numerous private foundations which have contributed to our Fund, such as the Bolton Foundation, The George W. Codrington Foundation, The Hankins Foundation, The S. Livingston Mather Charitable Trust, The McWilliams Foundation, the David and Inez Myers Foundation, the Norweb Foundation, The Sears Family Foundation, The Sherwick Fund, the Sindell Foundation, The Kelvin and Eleanor Smith Fund, and The George Garretson Wade Charitable Trust.

Before describing the golden anniversary celebration, a word should be said about a discrepancy in the dating of the School's opening — some accounts have mentioned October 1911, others 1912. The confusion results from the fact that when the School moved into its present building in 1938, records were apparently stored in available boxes with no logical order; the minutes of executive committee and trustee meetings were mixed in with old letters and other documents. Matters were complicated even more when these boxes were distributed around the house in odd corners, and the records of the first twelve years of the School's existence were not discovered until the early 1970s. At the time of the golden anniversary, these documents were still missing. The celebration was scheduled for October 1961 to October 1962, which was correct since October 1962 ended the fiftieth year of the School. However, in many publications of the School from then on, October 1911 was mentioned as the opening date of the Settlement. It was not until the early documents were found, that October 1, 1912, was incontrovertibly established as the opening date of the School.

The celebration of the silver anniversary had occurred in September, October, and November of 1937. The observance of the golden anniversary was extended over the *whole* of the fiftieth year, to wit, from October 1961 to October 1962. For the first event, a program and a tea, invitations were issued to members of The Music and Drama Club, the Lecture-Recital Club, and The Fortnightly Musical Club, three organizations which had provided scholarships and other assistance to the Settlement for many years.

The most original idea for the fiftieth anniversary, one especially appropriate for a music school, was the production of an album of recordings. Wilbur W. Merkel, a trustee, gave the School a taping machine that was used to prepare the records which began with a short introductory speech by Boris Goldovsky. Performances followed by faculty and outstanding students in works by four Settlement composers, Howard Whittaker, Herbert Elwell, Starling Cumberworth, and Bain Murray. Taking part were Theodore Lettvin and Andrius Kuprevieius, pianists, Josef Gingold (former faculty member), violinist; contralto Eleanor Pudil Anop, and the faculty string quartet. The album, produced by Boston Records, of which Mr. Merkel was president, was sent to faculty and board members, contributors to the endowment fund; radio stations; other settlements; and the Voice of America — a total of four hundred and seventy-five. It was not available for public sale, but anyone wishing one had only to contribute a minimum of five dollars to the Settlement endowment fund. The many complimentary letters and calls received proved the anniversary album to have been an artistic success of great public relations value to the Settlement.

In this golden anniversary year, the School had expert advice for its printed matter through trustee Howard Skidmore. An emblem was designed which included the slogan, "50 Years of Musical Service," a sketch of a mandolin, and the date 1911-1961 (which should have been 1912-1962). This was used for the catalogue and the calendar of events as well as programs, stationery, and miscellaneous pieces. Some of these items included two apt comments on music by classic authors: "Musical training is a more potent instrument than any other because rhythm and harmony find their way into inward places of the soul" (Plato); and "Music must take rank as the highest of the arts — one which more than any other ministers to human welfare" (Herbert Spencer).

A special part of the anniversary celebration was a series of recitals by former faculty members and students, all well known in the musical world as performing artists. Many, of course, could not participate because of previous commitments, but Boris Goldovsky, Jaime Laredo, Melvin Ritter, and Anthony Smetona were happy to do this for the School. As one newspaper reported:

> The Cleveland Music School Settlement annually gives a distinguished series of faculty recitals, and since this is the golden anniversary year for the Settlement, the recitals promise to be even more significant musical events than usual.

The first guest artist concert featured violinist Melvin Ritter and his wife, Jane Allen, as pianist. They were known professionally as the Ritter-Allen Duo, and their performance received splendid reviews. Herbert Elwell of *The Plain Dealer* (October 4, 1961) wrote, "The Cleveland Music School Settlement may take justifiable pride in exhibiting some of its most successful former students." Ritter, who had been a pupil of Felix Eyle from 1935 to 1941, had recently been appointed concertmaster of the St. Louis Symphony. The regular faculty recital in March of 1962 given by Theodore Lettvin featured the premiere of *Sonata No. 2 in D* written by Howard Whittaker to commemorate the Settlement's fiftieth birthday. Sometimes, as Elwell pointed out (*Plain Dealer,* March 7, 1962), works produced for such observances are far from worthy, but in speaking of Mr. Whittaker's sonata, he expressed himself as follows:

> This work had none of the dull earmarks of a *piece d'occasion*. It had rhythmic vivacity and a subjective undercurrent that plainly showed a search for meaning far deeper than that of music usually composed for a specific event.

In April 1962, Boris Goldovsky, former head of the piano department, returned to give a "laughter-studded" concert, as one critic described it. Actually, it was an illustrated lecture given from a teacher's viewpoint. The wit and humor which had characterized Mr.

Goldovsky's pre-opera talks when he was in Cleveland came to the fore again on this occasion and afforded the audience much enter-tainment. Jaime Laredo returned with his wife, who had studied piano at the Curtis Institute of Music when Laredo had been there. They formed a husband-wife team when they gave their concert in May and received excellent reviews.

Other institutions also helped the School celebrate. For example, members of the music faculty of Western Reserve University joined with the Settlement in March to present a chamber music concert in Severance Chamber Music Hall. The newspapers were extremely cooperative; besides noting all events, they published special articles, including one about Hyman Schandler, who had taught at the Settlement more than forty years.

At the end of the season, the board of trustees, the faculty, and the administration could consider the fiftieth "birthday party" as having been enjoyable both to participants and guests as well as effective in promoting the image of the School. On a bulletin board were posted many letters giving credence to this. At the annual meeting of the trustees, the president, Mr. Robinson, offered thanks to all for helping to make the year one long to be remembered. Though much attention had been placed on anniversary matters, it is well to point out that the School had nonetheless continued to function normally, but with a certain excitement because of the many outstanding artists who evidenced their love of the School by returning to participate in its special anniversary events.

Howard Whittaker, as director of The Orpheus Male Chorus, conducted the annual Severance Hall concerts of this respected group in 1961 and 1962, winning praise in both years. The concert in 1961, a salute to the centennial of the outbreak of the Civil War, was especially well-received. To judge from the reviews, it was a particularly moving event. The same year, Mr. Whittaker was asked to be the speaker at the commencement exercises of The Cleveland Institute of Music, from which he had graduated. His discourse was entitled "New Opportunities in Musical Careers."

The year 1962 was marked by the appointment of Burton Garlinghouse as head of the voice department. Mr. Garlinghouse, who had held this same position at Baldwin-Wallace College, took early retirement from that institution in order to join the Settlement. Within a short time, the voice department achieved distinction, and many new students enrolled. Mr. Garlinghouse persuaded Pauline

Thesmacher, Margaret Hauptmann, and Louise McClelland to teach at the School, thus creating an especially strong faculty. In subsequent years, other outstanding teachers joined the department: Penelope Jensen, Stephen Szaraz, Luise Cramer, and Violet Weber.

Mr. Garlinghouse felt very keenly that in order to have good vocal teaching, it was necesssary to have a capable accompanist for lessons as well as for recitals. Because the School's department of accompanying was no longer in existence, and the regular accompanist for recitals was unable to give time for student lessons, Mr. Garlinghouse established a special voice accompanying staff. These pianists were all professionals. Nancy Brittain was the first accompanist, and Dorothy Van Sickle came from Akron to serve as vocal coach; they were followed by such splendid musicians as J. Heywood Alexander, Enid Cohen, John Herr, Jerry Maddox, and Boise Whitcomb. This arrangement proved to be a valuable asset to the voice department.

The most stirring event in the 1962 school year, apart from those related to the anniversary celebration, was the visit to Cleveland of Nadia Boulanger, eminent French musician and teacher, who was the director of the American Conservatory of Fontainebleau. She had been the mentor of many well-recognized American composers, among them Aaron Copland, Roy Harris, Roger Sessions, Virgil Thomson, and others nearer to home, such as Herbert Elwell. On her visit here, she conducted two master classes at the School and gave a lecture at The Cleveland Museum of Art after which she was honored by the Settlement with a large reception. This year, too, Alexander C. Robinson, III relinquished his position as president to Dr. Lester G. Glick. With the close of the year 1962, the first half century of The Cleveland Music School Settlement had ended.

The School's achievements to date as a combined musical institution and social service agency and its enviable reputation had attracted internationally known musicians. The trustees had every reason to be optimistic about the future.

6. The Sixth Decade, The Sixtieth Anniversary and Beyond

PERHAPS AN APPROPRIATE MOTTO for The Cleveland Music School Settlement as it entered into its sixth decade could be taken from Robert Browning's *Rabbi Ben Ezra:*
Grow old along with me,
The best is yet to be.
The School's innovative approach to serving the community continued unabated, but early in January of 1963 planning was started for a monumental undertaking — the Cleveland premiere of Robert Ward's Pulitzer Prize-winning opera, *The Crucible.* This work, based upon a successful play by Arthur Miller, dealt with witchcraft trials in Salem, Massachusetts. It had been commissioned by the New York City Center Opera Company, and the first performance took place in October 1961. The circumstances which led to the presentation in Cleveland occurred in the fall of 1962, when Howard Whittaker and Dr. Lester G. Glick, president of the board, were in New York for a meeting of the National Guild of Community Music Schools. They both knew Mr. Ward, a native Clevelander, and wanted to attend a performance of his acclaimed opera. Very favorably impressed by it, they thought that the opera would serve admirably as the Settlement's contribution to the annual Cleveland May Festival of Contemporary Music the coming spring. Upon their return, discussions were held with the executive committee and Dr. Glick began a search for funds.

Howard Whittaker served as executive producer for the opera, an artistic triumph that led to the formation of Lake Erie Opera Theatre. Two performances were given in Severance Hall and members of The Cleveland Orchestra with Louis Lane, associate conductor, assisted. The production was in every way a collaborative effort of the Settlement and Orchestra. Many of the finest singers in the community were working with Burton Garlinghouse at that time, which was one of the reasons that the Settlement undertook this project; thus, it is understandable that a substantial number of the singers in the large cast were from the Settlement. Baldwin-Wallace College provided three artist vocalists from its faculty; The Cleveland Institute of Music was represented by a teacher and three graduates; and other singers came from several private studios. The stage director was Dr. Benno Frank of Karamu House; Paul Rodgers of The Cleveland Play House was technical director; Burton Garlinghouse was vocal director, and Louis Lane musical director. The performances were made possible by grants from the Recording Industry Trust Fund (which paid the Orchestra cost), several private foundations, and The Junior League of Cleveland, Inc., as well as by contributions from interested individuals.

Before the performance on opening night, a dinner was given in honor of Robert Ward by Dr. and Mrs. Glick, Mr. and Mrs. Robert Hays Gries, and Mr. and Mrs. Alexander C. Robinson, III. After the second and final performance, the trustees of the school hosted a large reception at the Settlement for the members of the cast and production staff.

The critics accorded the performance their highest praise. Frank Hruby of *The Cleveland Press* awarded the opera two resounding bravos: first, to composer Ward; second, to all the local musical and dramatic forces for their superb production. In the June issue of *Fine Arts Magazine, A Weekly Guide,* the critic, Patricia Ashley, commented:

> . . . it was proved to me last week that without calling on outside resources, Cleveland could, if she chose, produce operatic performances of a caliber worthy of respect anywhere. And if the composer of the Pulitzer Prize-winning opera was a former Clevelander, this just made one more Star in the Crown of a phenomenal local enterprise. There is much talk at the moment about a local opera company which does not seem unfeasible after this production.

In October of 1963, after the final audits of the opera had been made, the records showed that there had been a near-capacity audience on the first night and six hundred people had to be turned away on the second. The budget had been just under twelve thousand dollars; all bills had been paid by this time, and a meeting had already been held to discuss future plans with the heads of all participating institutions. It was the hope that, with the necessary financial support, more opera production of this quality could be undertaken.

Although the production of *The Crucible* was an *éclat* that brought much praise to the School, other events also enhanced its prestige. For example, in March of 1963, Howard Whittaker journeyed to Mexico to hear a performance of his symphonic work, *Two Murals for Orchestra,* in Guanajauto, Mexico; one month later, he received the Women's City Club of Cleveland Arts Prize in Music. In October, the Settlement was honored with an award for the promotion of American music from the National Federation of Music Clubs and ASCAP (American Society of Composers and Publishers). It was indeed a year of considerable media attention.

Expansion of the School's services and physical plant took place in 1963 and 1964. In trying to find extra room that was needed in the main school, the house committee toured the basement and came up with suggestions for converting eight possible areas into studios. Certain obstacles had to be overcome, such as partitioning, relighting, and replastering, as well as the funding that had to be obtained. But by May of 1964, all of these problems had been solved, and the areas had been converted into ten new studios for music lessons — seven of these had welled windows — and a large room for ballet classes.

Mr. Whittaker had informed the board in May of 1962 that he had received a petition from four hundred and thirty-eight families in the Mt. Pleasant area requesting that a branch of The Cleveland Music School Settlement be established there. The petition was the result of efforts by Mrs. Murtis Taylor, director of the Community Services Center of Mt. Pleasant, who at that time was the coordinator at the center for the extension program services of the Settlement. The proposition was presented to the Welfare Federation for consideration, and upon its approval, a request for a grant was submitted to The Cleveland Foundation. It responded favorably, and sixteen thousand nine hundred dollars was allocated over a three-year period for this new south side branch. A contract for the same length of time was entered into with St. Cecilia's School on East 152nd Street for the use of the rooms — coincidently, St. Cecilia was the patron saint of music. Gilbert Brooks was chosen as director of the South Side Branch, as it was initially called. A graduate of The Cleveland Institute of Music, Mr. Brooks had been conductor of the Institute's choral ensemble and director of music at Grace Lutheran Church; he had taught in the Settlement's extension program which was a particularly valuable experience. The faculty and staff were selected, some from the main school, others from the extension program, and the response at the opening of this branch in the fall of 1963 was beyond all expectation. As a result, the Settlement now provided service to more people than any other community music school in the country.

Clarification of the Settlement's purposes was effected by further revisions to the constitution and bylaws. As already recorded, some changes had been made in 1955. But, as always, the School was acutely aware of new trends and community needs, and it adjusted to them. The proposals were made, and the trustees' minutes of March 1963 recorded that a detailed study of the new constitution and bylaws had been completed. Final general approval was given after many recommendations had been adopted. The new article one, which gave the purposes of the School, now read:

> Purpose: To provide the finest training in music to children, young people, and adults with consideration of their ability to pay. To maintain a musical home where in addition to studying, there is an opportunity for listening to good music, and where enrolled students will feel free to come for advice and guidance with personal problems. To provide services in music therapy, extension of musical services to settlements and other social agencies, and to establish branches where the need arises.

By May of 1963, the extension program had completed ten years of service, and its director since the beginning, Richard Kauffman, gave an extended report. He explained that:

> The purposes had always been to bring sound musical instruction to members of each agency served, as well as to create the necessary conditions so that the members will obtain the joy derived from musical performance and music listening. As the needs in the various areas of the city change, so does the program.
>
> We have developed from music clubs and loosely knit groups, with uncertain attendance, to one of music and dance classes with a more regular attendance; groups and individuals in music therapy have also been serviced.

In contrast to 1952, we now have only two choral groups, no rhythm groups, but twenty-two piano and piano-theory classes, three musical events groups, nine modern dance classes, and the individual and group activity in music therapy.

Of note in 1963 is the establishment of the Charles V. Rychlik Memorial Fund, which was started by a trustee, Miss Dorothy Humel. The income from this fund was to be used for an annual scholarship in composition. Charles V. Rychlik, a violin teacher and composer of great distinction, who died in December of 1962 and in whose name the Fund was established, had not himself been connected with the School. However, he had had an important influence on the musical life of the city and was frequently among the audiences at Settlement faculty recitals.

Mr. Rychlik had been born in 1875 within the Broadway-Croton Avenue district, where the city's Bohemian population was centered, and he continued to live there until his death. A pupil of Johann Beck, he was only twelve years of age when he became a member of the musicians union and was also teaching youths in his neighborhood. At sixteen he was sent to Prague to continue his studies with the noted Otakar Sevcik. There he was graduated from the famous Prague Conservatory and later was invited to tour with the distinguished Bohemian String Quartet. A momentous day in his life was March 27, 1896 — while in Vienna, he and the other members of the quartet had the rare opportunity of being with three renowned composers. In the morning, they called upon Bruckner; in the afternoon they had lunch with Brahms; in the evening, the quartet's concert was attended by Brahms and Dvorak. Mr. Rychlik knew the latter well and had often visited his home in Prague.

When The Cleveland Orchestra was formed in 1918 under Nikolai Sokoloff, Mr. Rychlik was a member of its first violin section. Throughout the Orchestra's early years, and even into the 1970s a substantial number of the violinists had studied with Mr. Rychlik. Among his outstanding students were members of the famous Hruby musical family, three of whom had been members of the Orchestra from its beginning. In addition to their orchestral careers — subsequently all five, Frank, Alois, John, William, and their sister, Mayme, played in The Cleveland Orchestra — they were well-known teachers in the Cleveland community, having established the Hruby Conservatory of Music. Mr. Rychlik's compositions had been published in the United States and Czechoslovakia, and they were widely performed. One of his most important *oeuvres* was a twenty-five volume encyclopedia of violin technique, which was bequeathed to the Cleveland Public Library. Mr. Rychlik was active until the end of his life; thus his teaching career, from age twelve to eighty-seven, spanned three-quarters of a century.

In May 1963, a Charles V. Rychlik memorial concert was held in Severance Chamber Music Hall under the auspices of The Cleveland Friends of Music, Inc., the music department of Western Reserve University, and The Cleveland Music School Settlement. Dr. Jerome Gross, a Settlement trustee, a member of the Friends of Music, and a former Rychlik pupil, made the arrangements. A description of this concert by Ethel Boros in *The Plain Dealer* (May 8, 1963) stated:

> The modest, gentle, violinist, composer, and music teacher, who died last December at the age of 87 would have liked the memorial concert which honored him last night in Severance Chamber Music Hall. It contained beautiful music, played with devotion and artistry by longtime friends, as well as a fine tribute by Herbert Elwell.

Elwell pointed out that Rychlik was a musical link to the past, a man who had known Dvorak and who had shaken hands with Brahms and Bruckner. He was a blend of the American character of independence with a thorough sense of European culture.

Erno Valasek, another Rychlik pupil, who, when he was only twelve years old, had appeared as soloist with The Cleveland Orchestra under Artur Rodzinski and later became a first-place winner of the prestigious Leventritt International Competition, volunteered to give two concerts in memory of his first teacher. He came to Cleveland to perform in October 1963 at the Settlement under the combined sponsorship of the Cleveland Chapter, Society for Strings and The Cleveland Friends of Music. The programs for the two recitals consisted of three sonatas and three partitas by Bach for unaccompanied violin. As critic Frank Hruby said, "His technique was as flawless as that of anyone playing Bach these days," and as another critic remarked, "His former teacher would have had every reason to be proud of the achievement of his pupil." These recitals had attracted many new listeners to the Settlement, and shortly thereafter the goal of five thousand dollars for the Charles

V. Rychlik Memorial fund was completed. Through the very generous help of friends, the Fund has increased considerably in the succeeding years, so that the Rychlik Fund is able to provide scholarships not only for composition, but for string instruments and string ensemble training as well.

At the board meeting in October 1963 Mr. Whittaker reported that again, as in 1959, the School had received a gift of violins. This time the Settlement acquired eighty-six instruments through the interest of Harold T. Clark, a prominent Cleveland attorney. One of his clients not only purchased the violins from an estate and gave them to the School, but he added one thousand dollars toward their repair. The estate had been that of an elderly man of modest circumstances who had collected violins, mostly German-made; they were excellent for practice and loan to Settlement students and were a most useful gift.

Ever since the success of *The Crucible,* talk continued concerning a permanent opera company for Cleveland. In November Settlement representatives met with A. Beverly Barksdale, manager of The Cleveland Orchestra; Louis Lane, associate conductor, and Frank E. Joseph, president of The Musical Arts Association, which operates The Cleveland Orchestra. The Association tentatively agreed to underwrite all costs of the Orchestra and the use of Severance Hall. The Junior League of Cleveland, Inc., and several family foundations were interested in giving support on a three-year basis. In December, Mr. Whittaker reported on the progress in raising the necessary funds to establish this opera company. Commitments had been made for approximately thirty-nine thousand dollars and eighteen thousand dollars was still needed to help ensure three years of operation.

In April 1964, Mr. Whittaker could report to the trustees:

We are going ahead on the opera project. The checks will be received by May 1st, and there will be two productions each year. The regulations are being prepared. Dr. Glick is organizing the advisory committee . . . The Junior League will play a major role in public relations. Auditions will be open to all singers and institutions. In addition to The Cleveland Music School Settlement and The Musical Arts Association, the following institutions will be represented on the Board of Trustees:

Baldwin-Wallace College, Case Institute of Technology, The Cleveland Institute of Music, The Cleveland Museum of Art, The Cleveland Play House, The Junior League of Cleveland, Inc., Karamu House, Northern Ohio Opera Association, Inc., University Circle Development Foundation, and Western Reserve University.

A code of regulations for the opera project had been researched, and it was determined that because of matters such as liability insurance, another organization, distinct from the Settlement, had to be created to assume these obligations. In consequence, Lake Erie Opera Theatre was born. Nine of its original trustees were Settlement trustees, and two of these served as officers of the new organization: Miss Dorothy Humel, president, and Charles Klaus, secretary. With Howard Whittaker's participation as executive producer, the Settlement made a major contribution to the Opera Theatre's success.

The taxing role of Mr. Whittaker in Lake Erie Opera Theatre was detailed by Frank Hruby. He wrote in *The Cleveland Press;*

Howard Whittaker lined up the talent and saw to it that auditions could be held and when. He made the working connections between all the various artistic and cultural organizations that gave of their time, energy, and know-how.

Arrangements for the use of music — all of which was still under copyright protection — had to be made with due regard for royalties and fees. This is a factor frequently overlooked by the public in its consideration of modern or contemporary music.

Negotiations with the various unions had to be carried on to the satisfaction of all parties — musicians, American Guild of Musical Artists, stage hands, etc. Sets had to be designed, built and paid for, costumes and publicity had to be taken care of.

The leadership of Mr. Whittaker as executive producer of Lake Erie Opera Theatre and Miss Dorothy Humel as president of its board of trustees had many positive effects on the Settlement. Besides the obvious public relations value, a number of the Opera Theatre's trustees became interested in the School primarily because of its purposes; they were later elected to the Settlement's board and subsequently provided substantial support, both financially and in active involvement.

During the formative period of Lake Erie Opera Theatre, the days were particularly busy for Howard Whittaker. The trustees had been notified that two houses next door on Mistletoe Drive were for sale. Because enrollments were expanding and more space would be needed eventually, perhaps before too long, they were immediately interested. The head of special repair for the Welfare Federation had inspected both structures and reported that the city would permit the use of the red brick house for teaching and practice rooms and the white frame house for nursery school facilities on the first floor and a faculty lounge or custodial residence on the second. If the latter were to be used for the nursery school, the Kulas House could then provide a larger office for Richard Kauffman and a possible ballet room. The estimated costs of the houses were: forty-three thousand seven hundred dollars for the brick house, and twenty-eight thousand eight hundred dollars for the white frame house. After this report, the board wished to continue exploring the possibility of acquiring the two properties.

This year, 1964, in accordance with requirements of the Welfare Federation, a self-study of the Settlement was undertaken. The resulting recommendations were to obtain a full-time music therapist; to expand upon the current music and dance program for an arts-in-the-neighborhood concept by developing the interests and cultural opportunities of people in specific areas, and to develop the present pre-school instrumental demonstration program.

Contributions have been made to the Settlement from time to time by persons not having direct contact with it. They have learned about the organization's purposes and the work being done through publicity or from personal friends. This was the case in 1964, when the Settlement was the recipient of a large bequest from Nettie H. Cook (Mrs. Joseph E.), the granddaughter of Harvey Rice, the author and educator who reformed the Ohio public school system. She left a Steinway grand piano, a violin, and forty percent of her estate to the School, an amount which was estimated to provide eighteen thousand dollars annually. (Since that time the return has increased.) The income, the board decided after careful study, was to be used as follows: implementation of Welfare Federation wage and salary guides and payment of medical insurance for full-time employees; hiring of an arts coordinator to work in settlement neighborhoods and a music therapist, as recommended in the recent self-study; hiring of a full-time head of the string department; hiring of a full-time secretary for all clerical reponsibilities in connection with public relations, and payment to the special University Circle police force.

A comparatively new service which the School was providing was aid to the visually impaired through The Cleveland Society for the Blind. The Kulas Foundation in 1962 had approved a three-year grant for the Musical Events Group, and the September 1964 bulletin of the Blind Society carried this notice:

> The Kulas Foundation will make it possible for the Society to continue the popular musical events program . . . which is coordinated by several people. Miss Frieda Schumacher, of the Music School Settlement, arranges for the appearance of artists to perform at the meetings. Richard Kauffman, also of the Music School Settlement, plans programming for the group.

Several news items of 1964 are worth recording: Mr. Kauffman won a summer scholarship to the Akademie Mozarteum in Salzburg, Austria; Starling Cumberworth won the Women's City Club of Cleveland Arts Prize in Music; and Howard Whittaker was granted a six-month sabbatical leave beginning in November to be spent in Boca Raton, Florida. Richard Kauffman again assumed the duties of acting director.

At the board meeting in February 1965 Mrs. Marjorie Lentz, co-ordinator of the arts-in-the-neighborhood program, gave a report on her work. The trustees had allocated five thousand five hundred dollars from the Nettie H. Cook Trust for this project. Mrs. Lentz told of the splendid public relations that had been established through the Settlement's work with area churches, schools, libraries, and city recreation centers. Dr. Lester G. Glick announced that Mrs. Lentz and Mr. Kauffman were to attend the National Federation of Settlements' art conference in Philadelphia; this was sponsored by a governmental agency, the United States President's Committee on Juvenile Delinquency and Youth Crime, and Mrs. Lentz was to serve as a panelist for the conference.

At the annual meeting of the board in May of 1965, the trustees learned that the arts-in-the-neighborhood program (in cooperation with Merrick House Settlement) had attracted diverse groups and individuals through a variety of social and cultural activities. One such program was "The Spiritual Heritage of Tremont," which embraced thirty-seven different nationalities and their houses of worship as well as the parochial and Cleveland public schools. Buses took people from church to church, where special programs were held, including one which brought together people of Protestant, Roman Catholic, and Eastern Orthodox faiths. The program had been favorably received and the strengthening of communication in the area had been most gratifying.

In September, a workshop led by Dr. Richard Weber of Columbia University was held at the School. The various sessions were concerned with pre-school, culturally deprived, and retarded children. As a result of this workshop, a complete re-evaluation of the extension program was made as it related to meeting the needs of the culturally deprived child.

Two valuable gifts came to the Settlement in 1965 — one consisted of many orchestra scores from the music library of the nationally known Donald Voorhees, conductor of the Bell Telephone Radio Orchestra; the other was a collection of memorabilia of Almeda C. Adams, founder of the Settlement, who had passed away in September 1949. The Adams collection had been in the possession of Mrs. W. A. Jones, who had taken care of Miss Adams in her later years. Mrs. Jones, not certain what would be the best repository for these documents, gave them to Mrs. Vincent Patti, whom she knew and whose children were students at the Settlement. Mrs. Patti, realizing that this material would be of value to the history of Miss Adams's life, very graciously presented them to the School. There were letters and mementos from famous and interesting personages of the nineteenth century, a vivid addition to the record of this fascinating founder. The collection also contained numerous un-published manuscripts by Miss Adams, among which was a twenty-five-thousand-word novel entitled *The Romance of Kelley's Island.* This story reveals an author who seemed to be aware of all the things that sighted people enjoy, such as the beauties of nature. From this collection, too, it was learned that Mrs. Dudley S. Blossom, one of the original members of the Settlement's board, had quietly helped Miss Adams, especially in the last dependent years of her life. John D. Rockefeller had also befriended her, and on more than one occasion had driven her home from the Euclid Avenue Baptist

Church.

There were three significant changes in the operation of the Settlement in 1965 and 1966 during Dr. Glick's presidency: the expansion of the music therapy program with the hiring of a full-time therapist; the acquisition of the two Mistletoe Drive houses, and the affiliation with Rainey Institute. The music therapy program has not hitherto been mentioned to any extent, chiefly because its growth had been very gradual. By the 1960s, however, it had become a vital part of the School's work. Interestingly, about this same time, because of the increasing interest in music therapy, a degree program in this comparatively new field had been established at the University of Kansas.

In 1932, as noted before, Mrs. Ramsey, then director, reported to the board that the Settlement had been cooperating with various hospitals and clinics in planning treatment programs for unadjusted personalities. But the person who initiated music therapy in Cleveland in settings other than hospitals was Charlotte A. Ackerman (Mrs. Lloyd). She was a graduate of Colorado State Teacher's College and had been a schoolteacher before her marriage to a biology professor at Western Reserve University. Starting in 1948, she taught for sixteen years in the picturesque old stone schoolhouse on Euclid Heights Boulevard, officially named Superior School. There she instructed the Cuyahoga County classes for retarded children and was virtually a pioneer in the field of teaching the mentally retarded. Mrs. Ackerman tried various methods, studied the children and different curricula, and each year set up a program to fit their specific requirements. She was reported to have said, "The children inspired me and the needs of the parents sustained me when the going got tough." The sadness of the retarded pupils was one thing that impressed her greatly. This remarkable woman, though not herself a musician, soon saw the value of music in working with the retarded — it was apparent to her that when she led the children in song, their mood improved noticeably.

In the 1950s Richard Kauffman, the Settlement's extension program director, had also become interested in music therapy as applied to mental retardation, and he worked with Mrs. Ackerman and her classes. Mr. Kauffman, in introducing music therapy into the extension program, was helped in the beginning by the volunteer services of Helen Shapiro and Ruth Kumin (now Mrs. Michael Lamm). Mrs. Shapiro organized thirty-five volunteers to service all the Cuyahoga County classes for the trainable retarded; the work was expanded later, and five full-time music specialists were hired by the county board of retardation. It is of importance that by 1960, Cleveland State Hospital had an advisory board for music therapy of which Mr. Kauffman and Mr. Whittaker were members. The *Cleveland Plain Dealer* carried an article (November 6, 1960) quoting Howard Whittaker, who said, "Music therapy is a comparatively new field, where the shortage of trained musicians is acute. . . ." This same year, Mr. Kauffman gave a talk to the Cleveland Piano Teachers Club on music therapy to familiarize the members with the work that was being done.

At the annual meeting of the board in May 1960, it was noted that there had been an enormous increase in the requests for music therapy, but that much of this work had to be on a volunteer basis. Late in 1961 Dr. Juliette Alvin, founder of the British Society for Music Therapy, gave a lecture-recital at the School, and in 1963 she gave a similar demonstration for the annual conference of the National Guild of Community Music Schools which was held in Cleveland. At the trustees meeting of March 1962, Mr. Whittaker announced that he had recently spoken to the Smith Club of Cleveland about the Settlement's contribution to the music therapy program at Cleveland State Hospital.

In Mr. Kauffman's 1963 report of the extension program's first decade, he mentioned that music therapy was an established part of its work. Thus, this new use of music for mental health was gaining acceptance, and it was to enter into a new phase of development before long. In December 1964, advisory trustee Mrs. David Gitlin, a registered music therapist, gave the board a report on a particular music therapy project. She stated that Dr. Jane W. Kessler, director of the Mental Development Center at Western Reserve University (later to become an advisory trustee of the Settlement), had become interested in using music therapy in a nursery program for mentally retarded and emotionally disturbed children. Dr. Kessler felt that the Settlement's extension program could be of help in this regard, and that it would be desirable if Joan Silver (Mrs. Raphael) could be active with it.

In order to involve the Settlement there would first have to be a pilot program, a requisite in applying for a government grant. The executive committee approved the commencement of this program in January 1965 with a maximum budget of three thousand dollars and the hiring of Mrs. Silver, funding having been obtained from the George C. and Marion S. Gordon Fund through The Cleveland Foundation. By March, Mrs. Silver reported to the board that her time had been divided between the Mental Development Center and the nursery school of the Parents Volunteer Association for Retarded Children, the latter under Mr. Kauffman's program. She told that appreciable progress had already been made with many of the children, and with her guitar she demonstrated to the trustees some of the ways in which music can guide retarded children into group participation. Using her work thus far as a basis, an application was made to the United States department of health, education and welfare (HEW) for a grant-in-aid program through the division of handicapped children and youth bureau of educational research and development.

At the April 1965 meeting of the trustees, Mr. Kauffman spoke about the Great Lakes chapter conference of the National Association for Music Therapy which was to be held shortly in Flint, Michigan. He was scheduled to speak at this conference on "Music Therapy and the Community," which would describe the multi-agency cooperation in Cleveland. To be included in this talk was reference to the Harbor Light program of the Salvation Army for therapy to Alcoholics Anonymous which had been funded by a grant of eleven thousand five hundred dollars from the Kulas Foundation; the pilot project with the Mental Development Center of Western Reserve University; and the Musical Events Group of The Cleveland Society for the Blind. This last program was enlarged at a later date to include adults from the city's mental health centers as part of the rehabilitation program of the centers.)

In October of 1965, Mr. Whittaker reviewed for the board the recent developments in the project with the Mental Development Center. He reported that Dr. Max Mueller of HEW had reviewed the accomplishments so far in this preliminary program and was favorably impressed. It was hoped that the work would actually start in September 1966 at three agencies — the Mental Development Center, the United Cerebral Palsy Center, and the Community Action for Youth. Unfortunately, in April 1966 the trustees learned that HEW would not fund the music therapy request for mentally retarded and emotionally disturbed children. Such a setback did not daunt the trustees. Since a trained music therapist had been found to administer this program, and because a therapist was becoming a vital necessity to aid Mr. Kauffman in his work with other agencies, the board decided to hire Miss Anita Louise Steele and to secure the necessary funding elsewhere.

Miss Steele had been highly recommended by the person who has come to be regarded as the father of music therapy in the United States, Dr. E. Thayer Gaston of the University of Kansas. Miss Steele had a bachelor's degree from Florida State University and a master's degree in music education from the University of Kansas, both degrees with a major in music therapy. The hiring of Miss Steele was again an instance of wise planning for the future and the seizure of opportunity, even though a big risk was involved, qualities which had hitherto characterized board and staff members. As a matter of fact, the Settlement was daring in pioneering the field of music therapy services based in community non-mental health agencies. Miss Steele came in June of 1966 for a visit and started work in September, although the money for this project had not yet been found. The decision by the trustees to proceed was courageous, but correct; by October part of her salary had been pledged. Reports of the excellent work she was doing kept coming in, and Miss Steele more than lived up to the trustees' expectations, as time would further verify.

In November, Cleveland welcomed the annual conference of the National Association for Music Therapy which was held at the Pick-Carter Hotel. Richard Kauffman told the trustees of the Settlement's valuable contribution to this conference. He reported that Dr. Lester G. Glick, by this time the School's immediate past president, had been the keynote speaker; Dr. Jane W. Kessler had given a paper on the therapies used in the rehabilitation of retarded children; Mrs. David Gitlin and Mr. Kauffman had participated in a panel discussion.

And so it was that music therapy took its place in the work of the Settlement. Though its still more prominent and brilliant future was not known, it had already advanced, as had the Settlement itself, from humble beginnings to a leading position.

The second major event that took place in the 1965-66 school year was the acquisition of the previously mentioned two houses on Mistletoe Drive. The negotiations had dragged on since 1964, but a special meeting of the board was called for September 1965 to consider this purchase further. Dr. Glick, while president, had already spoken informally with the heads of the Beaumont,

Cleveland, and Kulas foundations to ascertain whether the School could expect their support for the purchase. They all agreed that the School should acquire the two properties, but it was their opinion that the Settlement now had substantial endowment resources of its own which might be used.

In August of 1965, Mr. Whittaker had prepared an analysis of the costs for repairing and equipping these houses as well as plans for their use. This information was presented to the trustees, and it was pointed out that when Kulas House opened, the enrollment increased by three hundred and fifty, when the basement studios of the main building were finished, two hundred and fifty new students registered. The projection, if these additional houses were acquired, was that an increased enrollment of nine hundred during a five-year period might be expected. The trustees were also informed that the owners of the houses had unfortunately raised the sales prices. After these reports and much discussion, the board established the top figures it would approve, and the conditions that had to be met, so that the Settlement would not be liable for any actions of the nursing home which was occupying one of the structures. There the matter rested, and no further action was taken by either side during 1965.

In February 1966 the transaction of the sale was beginning to progress, and Dr. Glick drafted letters to various foundations detailing all the negotiations, the status of the School's endowment funds, the services which the new acquisitions would house, and the increased enrollment anticipated. He obviously had made a strong case, because at the annual meeting in May 1966 it was reported that the Settlement had received twenty-five thousand dollars from the Leonard C. Hanna, Jr., Final Fund and twenty thousand dollars from The Cleveland Foundation toward the purchase, the latter having obviously reconsidered its earlier position. Finally, later in the same month, the deeds for the houses were signed, and a loan of eighty-six thousand dollars was received from Union Commerce Bank. By October, the loan had been reduced to twenty-eight thousand four hundred and forty-seven dollars. Once again, the School had expanded and could offer the community better and greater services.

The background for the third important change for the Settlement in the 1965-66 year was that representatives of Rainey Institute, located in a large house on East 55th Street near Superior Avenue, had approached Dr. Glick in 1963 about the possibility of Rainey joining forces with the Settlement; the request was repeated in 1965. Rainey Institute, which had been founded sixty years previously, had operated on a meager budget with a very small staff and was under advisement by the Greater Cleveland Neighborhood Centers Association (GCNCA) to re-locate or change its program. Goodrich-Gannett Neighborhood Center and League Park Center were nearby, and it was felt that there was duplication of services; also, there was much racial tension in the neighborhood, one side of Superior Avenue being predominantly white, the other black. That the affiliation with the Settlement would be of benefit to Rainey was self-evident, but would it be of advantage to the Settlement? At a meeting of the board in November 1965, Dr. Glick said that such an affiliation would offer certain benefits for the Settlement:

Rainey would be the perfect place for the extension program to carry on research.

The role that music was playing in the work currently being done with the culturally deprived was being expanded, and any new ideas that might evolve from the program with Rainey would be most welcome.

Staff with special qualifications would be needed for this work, but an excellent person was available as director.

A music therapist might also be used.

The trustees engaged in considerable discussion, and it was finally agreed that Dr. Glick should appoint a special committee to meet with the board of Rainey Institute to determine details of structural procedure for the affiliation. Obviously, there were innumerable details to be worked out by both organizations, but, by March 1966, Mr. Whittaker was able to report to the trustees that the Group Services Council special review committee of the Welfare Federation was ready to consider the Settlement-Rainey proposal at its next meeting. The Rainey building had been inspected by Alexander C. Robinson, III, of the Settlement board and Eugene Bittinger of the Rainey board, both architects, with a view to making estimates of necessary remodeling. There had also been a job analysis of what personnel would be necessary, and a tentative staff was under consideration. Mr. Whittaker read a statement that he had prepared for the Group Services Council, in which he pointed out the many advantages that would accrue to both the community and the agencies involved by this partnership.

At the annual meeting in May 1966, a report gave the status of further negotiations. It was a lengthy document which set forth the many ways in which the Settlement would work in this area of the city and detailed the estimates of financial requirements: twenty-nine thousand dollars for an operating budget and thirty-three thousand dollars to renovate the building. Also noted was the fact that forty-nine thousand dollars in anti-poverty funds, budgeted through the Greater Cleveland Neighborhood Centers Association, was available, and that several foundations were interested in assisting with the capital improvements. Listed in the report in addition to the traditional programs were: guitar for teenage juvenile delinquents, music therapy for slow learners, and several adult musical activities. All programs were to be interracial in order to help ease the neighborhood tensions.

In October of 1966, the agreement between Rainey Institute and the Settlement was completed. At a meeting of the trustees, Mr. Whittaker read portions from the document which set forth the purposes; he also explained a plan for the joint committee of three members from each of the two boards and the financial obligations of each institution. It was mentioned that "Operation Headstart" and another federal program with a budget of approximately fifty thousand dollars a year were already housed in the building; also, the Welfare Federation had been alerted to the fact that in three years, Rainey Institute might seek to become a financially participating agency. The agreement was approved, and Theodore J. Horvath, chairman of the Rainey board of managers, expressed thanks to the Settlement for the help and inspiration this new affiliation undoubtedly would be to Rainey Institute. He said that his board and staff would do their utmost to make Rainey a unique settlement house, one with a focus on the arts.

To Zandra Zerkle Richardson, the only director of Rainey since the merger, goes the credit for achieving many of the goals which the Settlement and Rainey had set. Mrs. Richardson was a graduate of Miami University in Oxford, Ohio, with a major in sociology and a minor in music. A former pupil of Alice Chalifoux, principal harpist of The Cleveland Orchestra, she had been the harpist for the Dayton Philharmonic Orchestra. Before her position at Rainey Institute, she had worked for the Cuyahoga County welfare department as a case worker in the Hough community. This background explains in part the reasons for her success at Rainey, although her own enthusiasm and devotion are even more pertinent.

It is appropriate to mention here that the establishment of the music therapy program and the successful affiliation with Rainey were due largely to the time and thought expended by Dr. Lester G. Glick on these two matters. The entire extension program had always been of particular concern to him, and his executive positions with the Welfare Federation's board had been very helpful to the School for many years, especially during his presidency from 1962 to 1966. As a child, he had studied violin at the Settlement, an experience which no doubt was responsible for his great dedication to the School and his insight about the way its purposes could best be accomplished.

In March of 1966, Dr. Max Kaplan, former director of the arts center of Boston University, and at this time advisor to the National Guild of Community Music Schools, came to Cleveland to review all phases of the extension program. He was extremely impressed by the large scope of the work being done, as illustrated by a map showing the many areas in which the program operated. In Dr. Kaplan's opinion, the Settlement's extension program was the most comprehensive of any with which he was familiar. He suggested, however, that more work could be done with the aged.

Matters which needed clarification by the trustees were the criteria to be used in awarding scholarships and the amount of money necessary to establish a name scholarship. The existing scholarships included the Josef Gingold, Nathan Fryer, Winifred Fryer, and Charles V. Rychlik funds. It took about a year for this matter to be settled, but a resolution was adopted by the board in April 1966, which stated in brief that:

    (a) Named scholarship awards be for talent only, not need.

    (b) Competition for awards be open only to students in the main settlement, its branches, and affiliate.

    (c) Written requirements for eligibility to compete and win named awards should be prepared and distributed by the professional staff of the School. No student could win the same award two successive years, but might be eligible in a third or later year.

(d) Named awards, memorialized by a separate plaque in the Settlement, must be established with a minimum contribution of five thousand dollars. (The plaque idea was never implemented. An honor roll of major contributors was installed in 1973 — accumulative gifts of ten thousand dollars being the criterion.)

(e) A Cleveland Music School Settlement tribute scholarship endowment fund should be established in lesser amounts with an appropriate plaque to honor persons, both living and deceased. A minimum of five hundred dollars should be required for each name added to the plaque. (This was changed to two hundred and fifty dollars in 1972 when a memorial scholarship endowment fund and a tribute scholarship endowment fund were established as an umbrella for these smaller funds.)

Also considered in 1966 was the selection of some tangible form of recognition for faculty and trustees who had given years of service. Mrs. Paul H. Oppmann, a trustee, worked on this matter, and the final choice was the presentation of gold pins in the form of a lyre — some plain, others set with different jewels, to designate length of service. The pins, given at a recognition party held in May 1966, to honor forty-seven faculty members, as well as some trustees, were presented by the president, Mrs. Webb Chamberlain. She had been elected in March to replace Dr. Glick who had to resign when he had been made chairman of the Welfare Federation's Group Services Council. However, at this party, since Dr. Glick had planned the awards, he was chosen to explain to the faculty and staff members that the pins were not in lieu of increased salaries, but were meant to give public recognition to those who had made the Settlement the outstanding community music school that it was.

Among those honored for long service were Howard Whittaker; four faculty members: Margarita Jolles, Alfred Kaufer, Hyman Schandler, and Margaret Sharp; and five past presidents of the board: Mrs. Clarence L. Collens, Edward W. Garfield, Dr. Lester G. Glick, Edward F. Meyers, and Alexander C. Robinson, III. A special award in the form of a gold spray of roses was given to Mrs.

Frank B. Meade, a trustee of long standing, who had done much over the years for the Settlement's Christmas parties. Mrs. Meade (Dora Rucker Meade) was a member of an old Cleveland family and at the time of this presentation was a widow. Her husband had been a charter member of the Settlement's board and had served as vice president. He was a noted architect, who had designed many of Cleveland's fine homes; he also had the distinction of having founded The Hermit Club. For many years, Mrs. Meade had supplied and personally put up the beautiful Christmas decorations, a gigantic undertaking which delighted the children, their parents, and everyone at the School. According to an article by Ethel Boros in *The Plain Dealer,* Mrs. Meade had always been a fabulous party giver, especially for children. "But at ninety," Miss Boros said, "she now confines her efforts to one big party, the annual Christmas party for three hundred children at The Cleveland Music School Settlement."

Mrs. Meade's attachment to the School was quite special, as was that of many trustees, each of whom contributed in his or her own way. Certainly, the Settlement could not have provided the services it did without their help, an excellent example being the gift of twenty-five thousand dollars which came in 1967 from Baltimore to endow five new annual scholarships. This had been arranged by an advisory trustee, Paul A. Unger; his aunt established the awards in flute, clarinet, oboe, piano, and brass in memory of her husband, Aber D. Unger.

Set against the summer program of 1967, all the usual day-to-day matters paled almost into insignificance. The Settlement became deeply involved in the Cleveland Summer Arts Festival, a city-wide project. It had front page publicity in all the local newspapers, drew forth considerable editorial comment, attracted the attention of many other cities, and interested the government in Washington. It was perhaps the School's most spectacular undertaking and its greatest social service program up to this time.

The idea was born one day in the fall of 1966, when Seymour Slavin, executive secretary of the Group Services Council, was conversing with its chairman, Dr. Lester G. Glick. Mr. Slavin remarked that much of the cultural activity in the city seemed to dwindle during the summer. He wondered why Cleveland could not have something like New York's Shakespeare in the Park. Dr. Glick's immediate reaction was, "Let's do it," and he put in a call to Howard

Whittaker. They arranged a meeting to formulate plans for a summer arts festival, but the time available to plan a vast program that would successfully take the arts to the people was short. Dr. Glick thought that the job could be done for several reasons: Cleveland had a strong neighborhood centers association; an interracial cultural arts center in Karamu, and a community music school, the Settlement, with a vigorous extension program of long-standing experience in the neighborhoods.

The idea was explored further when the Welfare Federation, through Mr. Slavin, formally asked Howard Whittaker to investigate the practicality of holding a massive cultural project in the summer. Mr. Whittaker was also executive producer of Lake Erie Opera Theatre at that time, but he felt very strongly that as the director of a community music school, he had an obligation to be involved in this period of crisis. It was suggested that orchestra, band, ballet, opera, and drama programs be held in ten areas around the city, and that neighborhood involvement might be obtained through settlement houses. Mr. Whittaker was to talk with Mayor Ralph S. Locher. Since New York City had brought its parks alive with a similar program the previous summer, Mr. Whittaker wished to consult Thomas Hoving (later to become director of The Metropolitan Musuem of Art), who had headed the New York venture. An appointment with Mr. Hoving was secured through the help of Sherman E. Lee, director of The Cleveland Museum of Art. The motivating factor behind the Cleveland festival proposal was the hope that such a program would help to avoid the riots and destruction that had already taken place in a number of cities, including Cleveland in 1966. Continued unrest had been prophesied for the summer of 1967.

After Mr. Whittaker had talked with Mayor Locher and the recreation commissioner, John S. Nagy, he received a letter from the mayor which gave hearty approval of such a festival and a promise of help from the city. Next, Mr. Whittaker went to New York with questions to ask Mr. Hoving, such as: Where did the funds come from? For what period of time was the program planned? What kind of shows were represented? How was the black community involved? In addition to his questions, Mr. Whittaker said that Cleveland was also planning arts workshops in the neighborhood settlements, and Mr. Hoving's response to this idea was, "That is just great. We were unable to do this in

New York because we don't have this kind of neighborhood
organization . . ."

In March of 1967, Mr. Whittaker reported to the Settlement's
board on the plans for the summer, and it was the consensus of the
trustees that the program would necessitate a tremendous effort by
many people; however, they thought that it could prove to be
extremely beneficial for the entire community. The prospectus given
by Mr. Whittaker outlined the following procedures:

     (a) Programs of mass audience appeal — involving
        such outstanding cultural entities as Lake Erie
        Opera Theatre, The Cleveland Orchestra, The
        Cleveland Play House, and others — would be
        held with the help of the city recreation depart-
        ment. Ten areas in the parks were to be chosen
        for these events, and the city law department
        guaranteed police protection. The city recrea-
        tion department was to provide the necessary
        physical facilities, such as chairs, lighting, and
        stages.

     (b) Art workshops in neighborhood settlements
        were to be carried out with the help of Karamu
        House, The Cleveland Play House, and The
        Cleveland Music School Settlement. Recruit-
        ment for the workshops was to be conducted
        by the city recreation department, the public
        schools, and the neighborhood centers.
        Through this program an enrichment experience
        would be provided for children, teenagers, and
        adults.

     (c) With contributions from foundations and the
        business community, it was hoped all programs
        could be offered free and open to the public.

     (d) The Cleveland Music School Settlement was to
        act as the administrative organization, handling
        all funds from foundations and the business
        community, and it was also to assume respon-
        sibility for contracting with performing groups.
        The director of the Settlement was to attempt
        to raise funds with the support and assistance
        of an advisory committee; he would also

procure the necessary staff to administer the
program.

It was evident from this prospectus that the trustees did not exaggerate when they concurred that the program posed a colossal task.

The Plain Dealer (March 29, 1967) carried on its front page an article by Robert Finn telling of the festival and what it would include. Lake Erie Opera Theatre, with The Cleveland Orchestra assisting, planned ten performances of its production, Puccini's one-act comedy, *Gianni Schicchi,* Louis Lane and Michael Charry conducting. A Play House company agreed to perform Shakespeare's *The Tempest* at all ten festival sites. Pop music and shows drawing on talent from TV's "The Upbeat Show" were scheduled for weekends. During the last three weeks, the students enrolled in the arts workshops were expected to give a "festival-within-a-festival," producing for the public what they had been working on during the summer in art, theater, dance, and music, both choral and instrumental. The *Cleveland Press* also had an article about the program the same day, and on the very next day, *The Plain Dealer* reported that the summer arts festival had been hailed by many here. It had drawn many offers of assistance from Ohio cultural groups, and Howard Whittaker had received innumerable calls from people who wanted to help. Great interest was also expressed by foundations which pledged support.

By May when money had been raised, a large portion of it by Group 66, an organization of young business executives interested in civic affairs, it became necessary, as with Lake Erie Opera Theatre, to form a separate corporation to protect the Settlement. The new organization was called the Cleveland Summer Arts Festival, and Dr. Lester G. Glick was elected president, most appropriately. He represented the Settlement on the new board, and other trustees and the institutions they represented were: Miss Dorothy Humel, also of the Settlement board (Lake Erie Opera Theatre); George D. Kirkham, II (Group 66); David F. Leahy (The Musical Arts Association, operating The Cleveland Orchestra); Mrs. Worth Loomis (Ballet Guild of Cleveland); John S. Nagy (City of Cleveland); Mrs. Frank H. Porter (the Welfare Federation of Cleveland); Mrs. James S. Reid, Jr. (The Junior League of Cleveland, Inc.); Robert D. Storey (Karamu House); Dr. George E. Theobold (the Cleveland board of education), and Arthur L. Vance (Greater Cleveland Neighborhood Centers Association). Another trustee, Robert D. Gries (son of the late Settlement trustee Robert H.), was named member-at-large, and he with Mr. Kirkham (both later elected trustees of the Settlement) were largely responsible for raising the funds. Mr. Whittaker was the director of the festival, and Seymour Slavin of the Welfare Federation was appointed as the coordinator of the planning committee.

The whole schedule of events was printed in *The Plain Dealer, The Cleveland Press,* and the *Call and Post* on June 7, 1967. By June 11th, it was reported that three thousand children and teenagers were enrolled in the free arts workshops. The day after the first performances in the parks, *The Plain Dealer* carried headlines on its front page, "City Arts Festival Brings Joy to 2,300." Pictures of the opening night crowds on both the east and west sides were also printed. On June 23rd, Mrs. Louden Mellen, artistic administrator of the Washington Opera Society, was in Cleveland on behalf of the Washington district commissioner to observe the Cleveland summer arts festival, in general, and the opera in the park, in particular; this was to determine if Washington, D.C., could emulate the latter. On June 24th *The Plain Dealer* commented, "Ballads, Jazz, Rock Highlight Weekend," On June 30th, *The Cleveland Press* headlined, "Children Enthusiastic over Arts Project." On July 1st, Ethel Boros in *The Plain Dealer* wrote:

> Hough became a cultural center last night as The Cleveland Orchestra, under Louis Lane's direction, dropped in for a visit at the old League Park, filled with 1,000 area residents — mostly kids — and the ghosts of lots of old-time ball players.
>
> But the big hit was the 50-minute opera, *Gianni Schicchi,* Puccini's melodious one-act opera.

On July 5th Milton Widder in *The Cleveland Press* reported that Robert Windeler, a *New York Times* writer, was in town for two days to write about Cleveland's festival. On July 6th the *Boston Herald* had an article about the opera. The producer of *The Tempest* noted that adults from the audiences often came backstage after the performances to thank the cast for coming to their areas. On the night when the popular Duke Ellington performed, it rained, but the large audience stayed to hear him. As one paper said, "4,000 Hear Duke Singin' Swingin' in Rain." By July 20th *The Plain Dealer* published an editorial which said in part:

> ... The Summer Arts Festival, born of despera-

tion to get something concrete going for the hemmed-in dwellers of the inner city, is turning out to be one of the best things ever done in Cleveland.

When 6,000 come to a park concert blending rock-'n'-roll and folk music, when 4,000 come in the rain to hear Duke Ellington, when opera and Shakespeare play in the Negro areas and are well received, when Negro performers appear in the west side and are well received, there is no doubt about the response.

When older youths and young teenagers dog the performers, asking how it is done, how does one break into this game — then one realizes how meaningful this program is.

Jazz musician Lionel Hampton came to Cleveland to perform, and he sought local individuals or groups worthy of obtaining a recording contract. Nine musical groups and individuals were announced as winners of the talent hunt conducted by Mr. Hampton. Selected from more than one hundred, the winners were given opportunities for recording contracts with major record firms. *Funny Girl,* a hit Broadway musical, the story of Ziegfeld star Fanny Brice, was presented at League Park in August. The production, which was to open the following Wednesday at the Wiley junior high school as part of the Sunshine Summer Theater, was loaned to the Cleveland Summer Arts Festival for this single performance, the costs being underwritten by the East Ohio Gas Company.

An article in *The Cleveland Press* (August 22, 1967) told of the work of Hugh Thompson, a faculty member of the Settlement and the head of the piano department at the South Side Branch. He had been, along with Howard Whittaker, a prime mover for the summer arts festival, "the most ambitious project ever undertaken by an independent group," as this article characterized it. Thompson had booked the talent for the programs of rock and roll, jazz, ballet, modern dance groups, and theatricals at the Cleveland parks. He had worked nearly every night from May through August, and though the pay was nominal, he loved what he was doing. This was understandable — the programs he arranged seemed to give a tremendous psychological uplift to audiences by exposing them to cultural events. There was no charge for any of the programs; and so, the summer went by and the crowds never stopped coming. It is quite remarkable that there were no unpleasant incidents.

As for Howard Whittaker's work of coordinating and managing the whole enterprise, no praise was too high. Special commendation must also be given to the following individual and institutions: Stephen Szaraz, who was to become the Settlement's associate director in 1968; Nathan N. Silverman, who handled all details pertaining to public relations; Anthony A. Granata, president of the Cleveland Federation of Musicians, who was cooperative in making arrangements with union musicians, both local and national; John S. Nagy and his entire staff from the city recreation department, all of whom gave their utmost support and cooperation; and J. Newton Hill, director of Karamu House, and Kenneth Snipes, Karamu staff member (later to become director), who organized and staffed the majority of the arts workshops — more than twenty-five hundred certificates of achievement were awarded to workshop students at the end of the festival.

Credit for fund-raising must be given to Group 66 and its president, George M. Steinbrenner, III; to Robert D. Gries and George D. Kirkham, II, trustees of the festival, as well as to industrialist Campbell W. Elliott (later to become president of the Greater Cleveland Growth Association). Of great assistance in organizing fund-raising meetings was James A. (Dolph) Norton, director of The Cleveland Foundation. There was splendid cooperation from K. Elmo Lowe, director of The Cleveland Play House, and his associate, Richard Oberlin (later to become director), as well as from Stuart F. Levin of the Play House children's theatre. Others who made noteworthy contributions were: Gilbert Brooks, associate producer of Lake Erie Opera Theatre; Robert J. Rice, supervisor of children's programs at The Cleveland Museum of Art, for his work with the studio classes; Louis Lane, musical director, and Michael Charry, associate musical director, Lake Erie Opera Theatre; George P. Carmer, business manager of The Cleveland Orchestra; Dr. Paul W. Briggs, superintendent, and Dr. George E. Theobold, assistant superintendent of the Cleveland board of education; Mark E. Talisman, administrative assistant to Congressman Charles A. Vanik; and Arthur A. Watson, vice president and general manager of station WKYC. At the end of the festival, the following appeared in a *Plain Dealer* (August 23, 1967) editorial:

It has been a magnificent summer spectacle and the applause should begin first for the men who dreamed up the idea for the long, hot summer evenings and who carried it out. Howard Whittaker, Seymour Slavin, and Dr. Lester G. Glick . . .

. . . It has been a rousing Cleveland plus — all because a number of people and institutions had faith in an idea which was written off at the onset, by some, as pure pipedream.

The close of the summer arts festival of 1967 was not by any means the end of the road. Not only was it planned to reorganize another festival for the summer of 1968, but representatives from numerous cities had written to Mr. Whittaker expressing a desire to promote such a festival in their own cities. Of importance, great enthusiasm had been kindled on a federal level in Washington, the result of which was an invitation from Vice President Hubert H. Humphrey to Mr. Whittaker, Seymour Slavin, Dr. Lester G. Glick, and George D. Kirkham, II, to attend a meeting in the capital to discuss such festivals. Also invited were Roger L. Stevens, chairman of the National Endowment for the Arts, and John W. Gardner, secretary of the department of health, education, and welfare. A second series of meetings had also been scheduled for New York in December to talk with David Rockefeller, representatives of the Ford Foundation, and others.

Mr. Whittaker reported to the trustees in February 1968 about these meetings. In Washington, he had attended a youth opportunity meeting chaired by Vice President Humphrey. With Mr. Whittaker at this meeting had been Seymour Slavin; Ralph W. Findley, the executive director of the Council for Economic Opportunities, and Mark E. Talisman, representing Congressman Charles A. Vanik. The meeting was also attended by members of President Lyndon B. Johnson's cabinet and by representatives of fifty other cities. The Vice President made a speech in which he stressed the importance of what Cleveland had accomplished, lauding the local effort that had produced such fine results by providing free entertainment and art workshops for thousands of people. The movie which had been made of the Cleveland festival was shown and brochures describing it were distributed. The best meeting of the week, Mr. Whittaker contended, had been held in New York with representatives of the Business Committee for the Arts, Inc., an organization devoted to the promotion and support of the performing arts, to which David Rockefeller belonged.

Cleveland went ahead with its own summer plans for 1968, and Mr. Whittaker met with representatives of the institutions and other groups involved. Fund-raising was planned, and budgets were drawn up; by May, the 1968 summer arts festival was going forward under the Cleveland: Now! program, which meant that festival funds were being collected through this one source. The National Endowment for the Arts had granted twenty-five thousand dollars to each of sixteen major cities on a two-for-one matching basis. By this month, too, Mr. Whittaker, who was serving as a consultant to Vice President Humphrey through the President's Council on Youth Opportunity, in addition to his work for Cleveland, had been assigned Boston, Buffalo, and Detroit to help develop their programs. These were all very troubled cities.

It should be noted that for all this extraordinary service and the national recognition accorded Cleveland, Mr. Whittaker was awarded two honors in the spring of 1968: one, a luncheon, was sponsored by the Ohio Arts Council and the Greater Cleveland Arts Council, which paid tribute to both Mr. Whittaker and the whole summer arts festival organization; the other, the Town Crier Award, was given to him for his far-reaching and successful efforts with the 1967 summer arts festival. It is of interest, too, that the second Town Crier Award, conferred at the same time, was bestowed upon a trustee both of the Settlement and of The Musical Arts Association, Mrs. Dudley S. Blossom, Jr., for her involvement in the establishment of Blossom Music Center, the summer home of The Cleveland Orchestra, which was to open in July.

The 1968 summer arts festival expanded its workshops program to include several additional categories of instruction. The Shakespeare play offered by the Play House was *The Merry Wives of Windsor,* and the Lake Erie Opera Theatre presented act one of *La Boheme* and Menotti's *The Telephone.* Having been pleased with a very warm reception accorded them in 1967, Lionel Hampton and Duke Ellington returned to Cleveland for performances, and other popular entertainers provided added luster to the second season. On the whole, the festival was again a marked success, though two events had to be cancelled because of racial troubles. At the end of the summer *The Plain Dealer* editorial (August 23, 1968) called the festival a "Big Winner" and ended with this comment: "The magnificent summer spectacle richly deserves continued support to remain an essential part of Cleveland summers."

Although the Cleveland Summer Arts Festival overshadowed all other activities of the Settlement in 1967, and to a somewhat lesser degree in 1968, it was not actually a part of the School's program, as was true also of Lake Erie Opera Theatre. These two organizations took up much of the director's time (he was working very long days every day of the week), but there were many benefits to the School without disrupting its regular activities. Music therapy, for example, had recently become a more significant part of the Settlement's work. At the board meeting in February 1967 it was reported that the Martha Holden Jennings Foundation had contributed three thousand dollars for the music therapy program; board members and others had given three thousand three hundred and fifty dollars; a family foundation had offered six thousand dollars; and forty-eight hundred dollars had come from services provided to Beech Brook, a home for emotionally disturbed children.

At the same meeting Mrs. Webb Chamberlain, president of the board, suggested that Mrs. Charlotte A. Ackerman, just then retired, be given recognition for her outstanding contribution to the development of music therapy in Cleveland. The trustees agreed that her dedication to the mentally retarded and her insight into the potential of music therapy should be noted; this was done by creating the Charlotte A. Ackerman post in music therapy of which Miss Anita Louise Steele was the first occupant. The announcement of this new post was made at a reception, honoring Mrs. Ackerman and Miss Steele, which was given by the trustees at the home of Dr. and Mrs. Chamberlain.

When Mr. Kauffman gave his extension program report at the annual meeting of the trustees in May 1967, he praised the work of Miss Steele and said that an article written by her had appeared recently in the *Journal of Music Therapy*. Because of the great demand for services in this specialized field, the trustees decided that the musical therapy program should move into one of the Mistletoe Drive houses, when it was ready for occupancy.

Considering the times in the late sixties, when racial riots took place and crime in general on city streets increased greatly, it was inevitable that the School should feel repercussions and be effected in some way. On Christmas Eve in 1966, all the copper piping (which was insured) was taken from one of the Mistletoe houses that had been recently purchased, but not yet occupied by the School. In 1968 the South Side Branch wished to move from St. Cecilia's school, partly because of vandalism, but mainly because the student body there was now derived from the Harvard-Lee district further east. More space was needed to accommodate the larger enrollment, and the South Side Branch relocated into the Harvard-Lee district in 1969. From this time on until he left the city in 1971, Marvin D. Hicks, a trustee, served as chairman of the South Side Branch committee and made a very valuable contribution to the branch's operation. The West Side Branch also wished to make a change in 1968. Its students no longer came from the immediate neighborhood, and the district itself had become unsafe — parents did not care to send their children by public transportation or even to drive them to the branch. Another factor was that many of the students were studying downtown at the Cleveland board of education's supplementary education center, where there was no charge for music lessons. As a result the West Side Branch was phased out in 1970. In all, the Settlement came through these trying days exceptionally well, especially if the impact of the summer festivals is taken into account.

Because Utopia is only a dream, the School also had a few unexpected happenings. In February 1968 fire broke out in the main school, the cause being faulty wiring in the basement. Damage, mostly from smoke, amounted to almost seventy-five hundred dollars, but it again was fully covered by insurance. Fortunately, those teachers who were displaced from the damaged rooms had been scheduled to move into one of the two houses on Mistletoe Drive, so no teaching hours were lost. Another experience of a different nature was the resignation in 1968 of Theodore Lettvin as head of the piano department. Though the trustees knew that he would be missed, they recognized that his reasons for leaving were valid. The president, Mrs. Webb Chamberlain, wrote a tribute to Mr. Lettvin which was framed for display. Andrius Kuprevicius, who had been with the Settlement since 1954, was more than capable of taking over for Mr. Lettvin and was made head of the piano department. He held a virtuoso degree from the State Conservatory in Kaunas, Lithuania, had also studied in Berlin and Buenos Aires, and had toured extensively in Europe, South America, Canada, and the United States.

In the spring of 1968, the Women's City Club's Arts Prize in Music was won for the third time by a member of the Settlement's faculty, Bain Murray, associate head of theory and composition. The arts prizes had been initiated in 1961. Also, at this time, Eileen Ingalls

(Mrs. Albert S., Jr.), a member of a prominent Cleveland family and a noted artist, generously presented to the School her three portraits of George Szell, Robert Shaw, and Louis Lane. She also donated many of her other paintings, a welcome gesture which did much to enhance the teaching studios and other areas of the various buildings.

The two houses on Mistletoe Drive were finally opened in April 1968. It had been almost two years since the deeds had been signed, but money had to be raised for their conversion costs. In addition, the renovation had been delayed because of problems acquiring permits from the city; by the time they were finally obtained, costs had escalated considerably. The Kulas Foundation had made it possible, among other things, to purchase pianos for the two facilities.

The brick house was named for Lucile and Robert Hays Gries in memory of the devoted trustee and his wife who had given unstintingly to the Settlement. The Gries House now accommodated the nursery school on the first floor, and the second and third floor studios were used for instrumental instruction. The white frame house was named for Margaret Rusk Griffiths (Mrs. Edwin S.) in honor of one of Cleveland's great music patrons. The Griffiths House became the center of the extension program, including music therapy. The dedication party was most successful — hostesses had made both houses bright with flowers — and the new furnishings that had been installed were viewed by an enthusiastic group of guests. Many trustees had contributed time and expertise to the acquisition and renovation of the two houses; noteworthy among these were Mrs. Willard W. Brown, who supervised the interior decor, and William H. Conrad, who provided architectural assistance. Mrs. Brown was in charge of refurbishing the other four buildings and spent much time in the selection of the furnishings. In addition, she was extremely generous in contributing to the expenses of these items.

Thus, through the continued dedication of its board members, the School had expanded once again. Approximately two hundred and twenty-five thousand dollars had been needed for this project (far more than originally contemplated), and Mrs. Chamberlain, the president, was largely responsible for the monies that had been received and others that would be forthcoming. She had literally grown up with the Settlement. Her mother, Mrs. Sterling Newell, one of the earliest trustees and now an honorary one, had also given meaningful service to the School as a volunteer teacher of voice in 1914 and 1915. One of the Settlement's greatest supporters, Mrs. Newell served as secretary of the board and had helped the School with many of its problems through the years.

At the end of June 1968, Mrs. Chamberlain relinquished the presidency of the board to Charles Klaus, an officer of Lake Erie Opera Theatre; through his close association with that organization, he had come to know Howard Whittaker and the Settlement very well. When Mr. Klaus presided at the first fall meeting, a resolution was adopted reiterating in detail the policy of the Settlement on non-discrimination because of race, religion, or creed. Though' this policy had always been in effect, it was the consensus of the trustees that a reaffirmation of it was expedient at this time. A new policy agreed upon was that beginning in the 1968-1969 school year, employment in the nursery school was to be limited to teachers trained specifically for this type of pre-school education.

In 1969, the trustees were faced with a challenging issue — the School was incurring deficits. At a meeting in January 1969, the financial condition of the Settlement was brought to the attention of the executive and finance committees: Howard Whittaker announced an anonymous gift of ten thousand dollars and said that that was the only good news he had. He then told of the seriousness of the mounting deficits — some money had already been borrowed from the endowment fund in order to meet operating costs. The members of the committees agreed that the endowment fund withdrawal represented poor management. Immediately, new financial policies were introduced. Stringent methods of operation were adopted in order to keep within budgets, and in February 1969, after a study had been made by the trustees and Mr. Whittaker, the following rules were adopted:

    (a) No new students on the sliding scale are to pay less than the teaching cost of the lesson given, excepting when necessary to fulfill a teacher's guaranteed contract.

    (b) Any registered student receiving student aid and not maintaining a "B" grade will lose the grant. This will result in a saving of scholarship funds.

    (c) Any registered student receiving student aid and not maintaining a "C" grade loses the privilege and must pay full fee if he wishes to stay in the school. For county welfare aid to dependent children (ADC) this means discontinuance.

(d) From February 1969, the ten percent courtesy grant to staff and faculty will be discontinued.

(e) From the fall semester, the registration fee will increase to eight dollars per year, an increase of one dollar per semester.

(f) For the fall semester, no student already enrolled is to pay less than the current fee he is now paying.

(g) For theory classes and nursery school, there are to be small increases in rate.

Later in 1969 came good news: the trustees learned that the Settlement had been remembered in the will of Mrs. Edwin S. Griffiths. She bequeathed the School one hundred thousand dollars outright and named it as the beneficiary of one quarter of a trust. With such friends as Mrs. Griffiths and others, the School was able, despite its operating deficits, to pay the outstanding balance on the building purchase loan for the houses on Mistletoe; to complete the interior decoration of various Settlement buildings; to pay its share of University Circle police protection, and to return borrowed money to the endowment fund.

The death of surgeon-violinist Dr. Jerome Gross in February 1969 was distressing news for the musical community and the Settlement, to which he had been closely connected, first as a student and later as a trustee for more than a quarter of a century. A scholarship fund for violin was established in his name as a permanent tribute to him. Dr. Gross had been an outstanding violinist having performed frequently in recitals and chamber music concerts throughout the Greater Cleveland area, and he also appeared as soloist with George Szell and The Cleveland Orchestra. To give other insights into his life is a quote from Bain Murray:

> Jerome Gross was a brilliant surgeon long associated the Mount Sinai, Cleveland Metropolitan General, and Women's hospitals. . . . Long the concertmaster of the Cleveland Philharmonic Orchestra under the Orchestra's founder, Dr. Karl Grossman, Jerry proved to be a tower of strength to this organization. . . . Jerry Gross taught himself

Russian, melted the psychological Iron Curtain, and became close friends of such Soviet artists as violinist David Oistrakh. . . . He was a supporter of the music department of Western Reserve University, The Cleveland Music School Settlement, and The Cleveland Institute of Music . . .

In the summer of 1969 there was again a summer arts program under the direction of Howard Whittaker. A newspaper account reported:

While retaining the basic features of the festival that have made for two successful seasons, this year's program has been revised and broadened to involve more neighborhood residents and to provide a showcase for local talents . . .

The festival is to be a giant cooperative effort by the city, the Cleveland board of education, The Cleveland Music School Settlement, The Cleveland Play House, the Greater Cleveland Neighborhood Center Association, Karamu House, The Cleveland Museum of Art, and other civic and cultural agencies.

Funds are being made available by the Mayor's Council on Youth Opportunity; Cleveland: Now!, the Music Performance Trust Fund of the Cleveland Federation of Musicians, and The Junior League of Cleveland, Inc.

An editorial appeared in *The Plain Dealer* (December 24, 1969) headlined, "Let's Have a Permanent Festival." By February 1970 a *Cleveland Press* item recorded that the summer festival was slated to continue, but that this time it would be under the aegis of the Mayor's Council of Youth Opportunity. "The original board of trustees, who worked generously to lay a firm foundation," an editorial in *The Plain Dealer* stated, "is disbanding." Hence, the city took over the festival. Also phased out in 1970 was the Settlement's involvement in Lake Erie Opera Theatre.

A new president, Richard S. Cole, was elected at the annual meeting in May 1970, succeeding Charles Klaus. It was in the fall that the West Side Branch was given up, as already mentioned. Luckily, though, something new appeared on the horizon to take its place — the Koch School of Music in Rocky River asked to join the Settlement as an affiliate. The request was studied and approved, and an application was made by the Settlement to the Kulas Foundation for funds to effect this proposal. The grant was subsequently made, and the Koch School became legally a west side affiliate of the Settlement in 1971. The original West Side Branch had been under the jurisdiction of the Settlement's board of trustees and was included in its budget. As a new affiliate, the Koch School had its own board of trustees that was responsible for the financing. Thus, the Settlement now had one branch operation, South Side, and two affiliates to which it provided program direction only, Rainey Institute and the Koch School of Music.

In 1970 the former nursery school was converted to a pre-school program; Sylvia Easley had taught in the former and was also its director during the last year, a position she now held with the new pre-school program. Before coming to the Settlement, Mrs. Easley had been associated with the Catholic headstart program and the Mather kindergarten. The primary purpose of the new program was to foster development of the individual capacities of the children enrolled. Educators, representatives of the medical profession, and others who visited this program all concurred that it was among the most outstanding in the city. The voice department also underwent change when Burton Garlinghouse retired. It was carried on under Pauline Thesmacher, a distinguished teacher, who continued to follow Mr. Garlinghouse's methods. That they were very effectual was attested to by the fact that quite a few students had achieved success nationally, several internationally, and that many others became excellent teachers. Some of the department's faculty were also very fine artists who performed in other cities — Penelope Jensen being an excellent example; she also made many appearances as soloist with The Cleveland Orchestra.

Further studies were made of the School's operation, and new policies were adopted which included increased fees for private lessons. Upon recommendation of Trustee Miss Dorothy Humel, group lessons at a lesser fee were instituted in order to retain as many students as possible. At the trustees' meeting in December, a board committee, which had been appointed to study the overall financial situation, made the following observations:

> It is the board's responsibility to deal with meeting operating deficits and to know why we have incurred such deficits. It is the board's responsibility

to see that there be a tightening up of the operation of the School so as to avoid annual deficits
. . . Our program of new buildings, new services,
methods of operation, expansion, etc. should be
scrutinized. . . . In the future we cannot have an
operational deficit. We should not borrow on our
endowment funds. In fact, we should replace the
entire amount already withdrawn. The committee
recommends that an immediate study be undertaken
. . . to prepare ourselves for a drive to seek
endowment funds and scholarship money in the
future, but not for operational funds. . . . We are
not justified in embarking on a drive outside the
School until we understand our problems and take
steps to avoid another crisis.

Among events of particular interest in 1970 were the
following: The National Guild of Community Music Schools met
again in Cleveland for its annual conference (planning for this event
had been done in conjunction with University Circle, Inc., and many
of the institutions in the area had been involved); the School was
the recipient of a portrait of Robert Hays Gries and Lucile Gries
from their children, Robert D. Gries and Mrs. Richard S. Cole, wife
of the board president; Mr. Whittaker was granted another six-month
sabbatical — this one to be spent in France — and Stephen Szaraz
became acting director in November; a tradition came to an end when
Mrs. Frank B. Meade, now ninety-five, was unable to supervise the
decorating of the School for Christmas, though she did help in the
selection of the tree.

An important development in 1970 was the approval of a six-
month internship program by the National Association for Music
Therapy. In March, a very fine account of this new program, written
by Wilma Salisbury, appeared in the magazine section of *The Plain
Dealer*. The article, which had been promoted by Trustee Mrs.
Hermann Menges, Jr., started out by saying, "The Cleveland Music
School Settlement is concerned with music both as art and as
therapy." It went on to tell about the instruction in music offered
to the normal children and the therapeutic use of music for those
with physical or mental handicaps. Explained in a clear and lucid
manner, it was splendid publicity for the School.

At the October 1970 board meeting, it was mentioned that there had been discussions with several colleges and universities about the advisability of establishing a program that would grant a degree in music therapy. There was general agreement that this idea should be pursued. The president of the board, Mr. Cole, commented at this meeting that the many facets of the music therapy field were exciting, and the Settlement's involvement in it was something of a snowballing phenomenon. The success was due primarily to the great ability of Anita Louise Steele, the head of this program. She had been honored by the Florida State University school of music, where she was the recipient of the Ella Scoble Opperman Citation for Leadership in Music Education, the only music therapist ever to have received this award.

In March of 1971, an encomium was presented to Margaret DeLuca as the first music therapy intern to complete an internship in a community-based program at The Cleveland Music Settlement. Miss DeLuca expressed her gratitude for the superior training she had received from Miss Steele and Miss Helen Jorgensen, associate had of the program, and for the opportunity to be involved in community planning sessions with the music therapy staff. *The Cleveland Press,* in an article by Frank Hruby (March 17, 1971), reported that Miss DeLuca "leaves town today, but not before we ask her — and the Music School Settlement — to take a bow for the work they have done over the past six months. . ." Shortly thereafter, a grant of forty-five hundred dollars was received from The Cleveland Foundation for music therapy equipment, and a grant of ten thousand dollars from the Kulas Foundation was made to enlarge the music therapy staff.

Before considering further the years 1971 and 1972, statistics regarding the racial, ethnic, and socio-economic composition of the Settlement's enrollment should be mentioned. They were presented to the trustees in May 1970 at the annual meeting; they appear in Appendix I.

The death of advisory trustee George Szell in July should also be noted. At the September 1970 meeting of the board, Mr. Cole spoke of the passing of Mr. Szell. He was not only a loss to the Settlement, but as musical director of The Cleveland Orchestra, his death was an enormous blow to the city and world. Under his leadership the Orchestra had been acclaimed in the great music capitals abroad, where The Cleveland Orchestra came to personify the very highest of musical standards. Mr. Szell had always been most cooperative with Howard Whittaker in discussing matters that directly concerned the Settlement, as well as others that concerned the musical life of the city as a whole. Thus, it was most fitting that a memorial scholarship endowment fund carrying his name was established at a later date.

By 1971, after careful work on the budget, the treasurer's report presented a brighter picture. It should be remembered that most schools in the early 1970s were experiencing financial problems, primarily because of inflation. But with the constant vigilance that the board of trustees and the administration gave to this matter, there was every prospect that the School would overcome its problems, just as it had those of the depression in the 1930s.

Following a study by community leaders in 1971, the function of allocating funds was transferred from the Welfare Federation to the United Torch Services. The Settlement continued as a financially participating member of the United Torch and became a non-financially participating member of what had been the Welfare Federation; the latter was reconstituted as the Federation for Community Planning.

It was natural that the Settlement, with a community-oriented focus, should participate in the Cleveland Arts '71 program. This venture, involving many Cleveland institutions as well as Oberlin College and Kent State University, took the place of the Cleveland May Festival of Contemporary Music which had not been able to continue. Gilbert Brooks, director of the South Side Branch, was the director of Cleveland Arts '71. The Settlement's contribution was a faculty recital, the main feature being a cycle of five songs composed by faculty member and former Cleveland Orchestra horn player, William Slocum.

In 1971, the Settlement was attracting considerable attention through its pre-school program. The increasing enrollment and the new equipment, which had been purchased in the fall of 1970, plus the utilization of new teaching methods, created an enriching and stimulating learning environment for the children. Evidence of the program's quality was the approval given by the urban studies program for students from the colleges of Hiram, Oberlin, Heidelberg, and Wooster to work full-time for one semester with the pre-school staff. At the end of this period, the students were to receive fifteen hours credit for their work. Also, numerous students from Cuyahoga Community College, and the universities of

Cleveland State, Kent State, and Case Western Reserve observed or worked in the pre-school of the Settlement during the 1970-1971 school year.

In the fall of 1971, there were several interesting programs, some with guest artists, others with faculty members. Included in these was a benefit in October by the Orchestra Michelangelo di Firenze, a chamber music ensemble touring this country. Another guest-artist recital was by Carol Sindell (the child violin prodigy who had studied at the Settlement) and her husband, cellist Daniel Domb, a new member of The Cleveland Orchestra. The Classical Guitar Society and the Settlement joined together to present a benefit concert; one of the compositions performed was quite unusual — tonal effects were created by methods such as sliding a water glass up and down the guitar fingerboard. In November, the newly formed Cleveland Orchestra String Quartet gave a concert at the Settlement. Included in this ensemble were two faculty members, the concertmaster and principal cellist of the Orchestra, Daniel Majeske and William Stokking.

Added to the ballet and harpsichord departments, which had entered the curriculum of the School in 1966 and 1967, respectively, was jazz piano and improvisation, a 1971 adjunct under Dr. Joseph A. Howard. Jazz pianist, composer, and arranger Joe Howard, as he was known professionally, received the doctorate in music from Case Western Reserve University.

Although other years had witnessed changes in the Settlement, they could not compete in this respect with 1972, in which a dynamic reorganization was made. It had become evident that, although economy measures had been adopted and fees had been increased, these were not sufficient for the Settlement to continue providing its many services to the Greater Cleveland community without incurring further deficits. Actions were taken to bring the work of the School to the attention of the general public and to involve more individuals directly in a board capacity. These measures were taken at the suggestion of the new president of the board, elected in May of 1972, Miss Dorothy Humel. She was herself a musician, having studied with José Iturbi, and had performed as piano soloist with The Cleveland Orchestra at twilight concerts in Severance Hall and at pop concerts in Public Hall. One appearance was with Arthur Fiedler, as guest conductor, when she was president of The Women's Committee of The Cleveland Orchestra. Also, she had had wide experience as a trustee and officer of other musical institutions in the community as well as of a national group, having been the only Cleveland woman ever to have served as president of the Association of Women's Committees for Symphony Orchestras.

The organizational changes were stated in the 1972-73 self-study — such a study, as mentioned earlier, had been carried on from time to time but was now required periodically for readmission to United Torch Services. The listings were as follows:

> (a) In April 1972, the code of regulations and the articles of incorporation were amended to provide for a larger board of trustees, a new women's council, and a voting membership to include non-trustees.

> (b) In May 1972, twenty new term trustees (formerly regular trustees) were elected, and by December 1972 seven new advisory trustees were elected.

> (c) In June 1972, the bylaws for the new women's council were approved, and in accordance with these bylaws, the board of trustees elected the initial officers and trustees of the council.

> (d) The executive committee was increased in size from eleven to twenty. Standing committees were increased in number from ten to fifteen, new ones were in the areas of community enrichment, membership, personnel, program, and visiting.

> (e) Permission was requested of United Torch Services in May for a membership solicitation of private individuals; this was granted in November 1972. A friends membership was created entitling donors of twenty-five dollars or more to membership in the corporation and its privileges, including voting.

These changes marked important milestones in the history of The Cleveland Music School Settlement. It was appropriate that they be instituted in the fall school term of 1972, the time of the Settlement's sixtieth anniversary; also, by a happy coincidence, the same term was the culmination of twenty-five years of service by Howard Whittaker. To celebrate these events, the trustees chose to hold an open house on a Sunday afternoon in September in observance of the School's anniversary followed by a dinner for invited guests in honor of Mr. Whittaker. The idea of an open house was especially fitting, since the School could now really claim a campus. All the buildings were on view for the open house, and the new women's council, under the guidance of its first chairman, Mrs. Hermann Menges, Jr., assisted by the members' husbands, made all arrangements for refreshments in various buildings. The invitation list was comprised of trustees, faculty and staff members, representatives from University Circle institutions and United Torch Services, trustees of organizations affiliated with the Settlement, other civic leaders, and contributors including foundation representatives.

Co-chairmen of the dinner were Mrs. Newton D. Baker, III, and Mrs. Dudley S. Blossom, Jr. It is significant that these two trustees, who were playing a leading role in the sixtieth anniversary observance of the Settlement, had direct ties to two original trustees, Newton D. Baker and Mrs. Dudley S. Blossom. Too, as noted earlier, Mrs. Baker's mother-in-law had been one of the first volunteer teachers.

The afternoon and evening celebrations were most successful. Howard Whittaker was quoted as saying in an article in *The Plain Dealer* (September 11, 1972), "The people began arriving at 2:30 and they never stopped." At the dinner in the evening, Miss Dorothy Humel, the board president, unveiled a portrait of Almeda C. Adams, which had been painted and contributed by Eileen Ingalls, noted Cleveland artist who had previously been generous to the School. As a gift from the trustees, an engraved silver box was presented to Howard Whittaker, and Miss Humel announced that a fund within the new tribute scholarship endowment had been established by a trustee in his honor. In her remarks about the sixtieth anniversary, she commented:

> From the day the Settlement opened its doors, this School has moved forward, and it has blossomed and flowered into a highly respected institution of great stature. Today, The Cleveland Music School Settlement is the largest community music school in the country. Through the years, countless individuals have contributed to its extraordinary development — professional staff members in establishing and maintaining high

standards of excellence, and ever so many generous friends in giving so willingly of their time and financial support. That the School now provides services and guidance to thousands in more than fifty locations throughout this entire area is a tribute to all those who have believed in its basic philosophy, particularly the ones who were responsible for its founding.

In connnection with the event, many communications were received from individuals and institutions including The Cleveland Institute of Music; the Federation of Catholic Community Services; the Federation for Community Planning; the Ohio Music Teachers' Association; United Torch Services; Case Western Reserve University; the Cleveland Federation of Musicians; Edward W. Garfield, former president of the board; Mrs. Mabel McCallip Paul, sister of Emily McCallip Adler (former director of the School); and Mrs. Thomas Munro, an honorary trustee. Also, at this time, there was much publicity about Howard Whittaker, the executive director, as he was now designated (this to differentiate him from the directors of the extension program, South Side Branch, Rainey Institute, and Koch School of Music). Profiles of his life and articles on the Settlement appeared in *The Plain Dealer* and *The Cleveland Press* by Robert Finn and Frank Hruby, respectively; and there was a salute to Mr. Whittaker by radio station WCLV in two broadcasts, one local, featuring his music, and the other national, with an interview. It was evident that the School and Mr. Whittaker had earned great respect, both in Cleveland and across the nation.

In November 1972, the Musical Events Group of the extension program observed its twelfth year; this group, which had met faithfully in the evenings, was composed of blind people and those who had been mentally ill. Trustee Mrs. W. Raymond Barney, who had been particularly devoted to this phase of Richard Kauffman's work, provided refreshments and planned all the details to make the celebration a joyous occasion. In subsequent years, she continued her generosity by instituting Christmas parties for this unique group as well as for the children enrolled in the music therapy program.

In the spring of 1973 still another anniversary was noted, that of Mr. Kauffman's twentieth year as director of the extension program. Under the guidance of a trustee, Mrs. J. Heywood Alexander, chairman of the extension program committee, the anniversary observance paid tribute to Mr. Kauffman for his creative and distinguished leadership that had added immeasurably to the Settlement's reputation. A gift was presented to Mr. Kauffman in appreciation of his service, and it was announced that a new fund carrying his name had been established within the tribute scholarship endowment by a trustee. At the reception preceding the dinner, extension program volunteers were given awards, and Ralph J. Perk, mayor of the city of Cleveland, presented a congratulatory proclamation naming April 8, 1973 "Cleveland Music School Settlement Day." After the buffet supper, an address was given by Charles Mark, executive director of the National Guild of Community Music Schools, who had come from Washington, D.C. especially for the occasion.

Besides the organizational changes already quoted, the self-study states that there were many new developments undertaken in the main school, its branch, and two affiliates, all planned to make the Settlement a more effective institution and to assist in obtaining additional financial support. As written in the study, these developments were as follows:

MAIN SCHOOL

A new logo, catalogue, and program format were designed.

The history of the Settlement was being written.

A memorial scholarship endowment fund and a tribute scholarship endowment fund were established, the names of those honored by accumulated contributions of two hundred and fifty dollars or more to be sub-listed under these two general endowment funds. An honor roll of major contributors (accumulated gifts of ten thousand dollars or more) was prepared to be placed in a prominent place at the main school.

A part-time director of communications and development was hired; a newsletter was started (the same idea as the bulletin published for several years beginning in 1919).

Master classes were initiated, the first ones having been given by the internationally known musicians, John Browning and Isaac Stern; these classes were open to Settlement students, faculty, trustees, and the general public.

A highly successful innovation: audiences at all faculty recitals were invited by the women's council for refreshments and a social hour with the artists.

Faculty recitals were taped for re-broadcast on station WCLV.

The Congress of Orchestral Instruments was co-sponsored by The Cleveland Orchestra, the Cleveland Federation of Musicians (Music Performance Trust Fund), the Cleveland Public Schools, and the Settlement. Students shared a week of music making with members of The Cleveland Orchestra. This included sectional rehearsals at the Settlement with Orchestra members and two rehearsals, playing side by side with The Cleveland Orchestra in preparation for the culmination of the congress — two educational concerts with audiences of young people in attendance at Severance Hall.

A major outreach to the community came through the Settlement's new community enrichment committee. The Settlement entered into a joint program with University Circle, Inc., the purposes being to bring the activities of Circle institutions to the residents (adults and children) of neighborhoods contiguous to the Circle; to bring these neighbors to the Circle institutions; to find out their needs in the arts; to implement ways in which the Circle institutions could meet these needs. Talks were held with University Circle representatives during the summer of 1972, and the program began operating in January 1973, funding being provided through a grant to University Circle, Inc., by The George Gund Foundation. The Settlement's community enrichment committee, Mrs. William C. Treuhaft, chairman, acted in an advisory capacity, and Gilbert Brooks, former director of the Settlement's South Side Branch, was named the director of University Circle Center for Community Programs. Some of the accomplishments of this program in its first months of operation: three thousand two hundred and forty-three persons were provided with services; thirty programs were sent to eleven schools in the area; a new series of Sunday afternoon community enrichment recitals, with programs planned for family attendance, were given in the recital hall of the School; tours of three musical institutions in the Circle and the Church of the Covenant were scheduled; open rehearsals of The Cleveland Orchestra and its chorus were made available to visiting groups; The Cleveland Museum of Art and The Cleveland Institute of Art offered art and appreciation of art instruction; programs were taken into the community, including Amasa Stone House (a home for the aged); Dalcroze eurythmic instruction was given to blind children at The Cleveland Society for the Blind; and a music teacher was provided for three elementary schools that had no music programs.

A professional music librarian, Miss Isabel Marting, (later to become an advisory trustee), former head librarian at The Julliard School of Music, and sister of Trustee Mrs. William C. Treuhaft, consented to make a survey of the Settlement's library; she made specific recommendations concerning the library's future uses by the community, if funds could be found to reopen it.

A complete review of the Settlement's insurance policies was made. Through the help of a new trustee, B. Scott Isquick, all properties, exterior and interior, were reappraised. This resulted in a more realistic insurance coverage reflecting the value and use of the properties.

EXTENSION PROGRAM

The ten neighborhood centers to which the Settlement provided services were asked to appoint a representative to serve on an extension program committee with Richard Kauffman, director of the extension program, and Mrs. Ruth T. Lucas, trustee of the Settlement. This committee agreed at its first meeting in the fall that assistance to the neighborhood centers program should be given highest priority. Meetings were held with representatives of The George Gund Foundation, and an application for a grant was submitted for a special project concerning this program. The Foundation gave favorable consideration to the request, and a grant of twenty-two thousand six hundred and eighty-two dollars was approved for a three-year program at the Community Services Center of Mt. Pleasant, East End Neighborhood House, Friendly Inn, Garden Valley Neighborhood House, Glenville Community Center, Goodrich-Gannett Neighborhood Center, League Park Center, Merrick House Settlement, University Settlement, and West Side Community House. It included the training of teaching assistants, selecting teenagers who had excelled in the present programs at these institutions. The second step of the program was to extend the Settlement's present teaching services for a six-week period in the summer, using the trainees as teachers in primary education for which they were to be compensated. (This program became known as Teens in Training or T-'n-T.)

Robert Finn, music critic of *The Plain Dealer* (later an advisory trustee of the Settlement), was requested to write an article highlighting the need for pianos for talented students who did not have instruments in their homes and were so motivated that they went to the neighborhood centers to practice. This article resulted in the contribution of twenty-one pianos in good condition, and the Settlement secured a grant from the Robert and Lucile Gries Charity Fund to cover the cost of moving them to the homes of students.

MUSIC THERAPY

Trustees were invited to observe sessions given by music therapists.

A new institute for music therapy, offering

introductory type courses, was established in response to a mounting interest in this field expressed by music educators and teachers as well as students considering future career opportunities. Twenty-eight students were enrolled in the first class and the success of the institute prompted renewed discussions with representatives of colleges and universities to form a consortium for a future training program in which students of these institutions would participate.

PRE-SCHOOL PROGRAM
In response to many requests, a new kindergarten program was started in September of 1972.

SOUTH SIDE BRANCH
An endowment fund for scholarships at the branch was created by a new trustee and added to by others.

A Sunday afternoon recital series was introduced, and the women's council provided refreshments for the audiences.

A new parents' association was formed.

A meeting of the board of trustees was held for the first time at the branch.

KOCH SCHOOL OF MUSIC
A women's council was created to assist in fund-raising, in forming a library, and other activities.

RAINEY INSTITUTE
A luncheon was held at Rainey to interest new people, primarily business men of the area, in the work of this agency.

A Sunday afternoon recital series was begun, and refreshments for the social hours following were provided by a Settlement trustee.

Though all these new undertakings were in the limelight during the school year 1972-1973, certain typical features and events of special interests to the Settlement family in 1972 should not be overlooked. They are described here in chronological order.

The trustees were very pleased when several concerts were given for the benefit of the Settlement's two affiliates, Rainey Institute and the Koch School of Music; these events were initiated by the affiliates' representatives. In January, a guitar recital was given by the world renowned Andres Segovia at Severance Hall and was co-sponsored by the Dick Lurie Guitar Studio and WCLV; from this event, the sum of thirty-six hundred dollars was raised for Rainey Institute. The other two benefits were for the Koch School of Music.

In March, Jill Cohen, a daughter of faculty members Mr. and Mrs. Frederick E. Cohen, and a Settlement student, won the fourteenth annual string contest sponsored by the Cleveland Federation of Musicians. The following month there was good news, too, about Danny Cason, a black fourteen-year-old student at Rainey Institute, who received a scholarship to the Idyllwild School of Music in California. Brought to the attention of the trustees at the April board meeting was the pre-school instrumental demonstration program. The self-study of 1964 had strongly urged that this program be expanded, and the report to the board concerning the development of this program demonstrated that such recommendations were heeded by the School's administration.

In May the Settlement joined again in the Cleveland arts program, Cleveland Arts '72, with participation in two concerts. The first, presented at the School, was composed of contemporary music and was performed by students from the main school, the South Side Branch, the Koch School of Music, Rainey Institute, and the extension program. It was a very rewarding experience for these students from the different areas of the community to perform together. For the second concert, the Settlement collaborated with The Cleveland Museum of Art in presenting a tribute to Stravinsky that took place in the Museum's new Gartner Auditorium.

Pride in the achievements of its members could be taken by the board in June. A trustee of long-standing, Mrs. William C. Treuhaft, and her husband were presented with a national award by the National Conference of Christians and Jews. Mrs. Leland Schubert, a new trustee, and her husband, were given the 1972 Benedict Rodman Award by John Carroll University.

Old friends of the School were remembered in October 1972 by visits from Miss Dorothy Humel, president, and Howard Whittaker. They called upon James Savage, director of the School of Fine Arts (formerly the Willoughby Fine Arts Center), who had been brought to Cleveland originally by the Settlement as a faculty member. The School had recently moved to a new and well-designed facility on the grounds of Andrews School in Willoughby and was a very active institution that was bringing music and other arts to its community. Miss Humel and Mr. Whittaker also went to see Mrs. Frank B. Meade. Now ninety-seven and frail, she was still eager to hear all details of the anniversary celebrations. Unfortunately, this was the School's last communication with Mrs. Meade; she died in the early part of 1973 after having given more than fifty years of service to the Settlement. To recognize her contributions, the board of trustees adopted a memorial resolution in May. By July of 1973, the Dora Rucker Meade Fund had been established within the memorial scholarship endowment fund (not to be confused with the George Anna Meade Fund established by the musicians union earlier in 1973).

At the South Side Branch in November 1972, an inspiring recital was given by two outstanding black musicians, cellist Donald White and his wife Dolores, a pianist. Mr. White, a member of The Cleveland Orchestra, taught at the main school; his wife was a former member of the faculty. A large and enthusiastic audience was present, including many residents of the Harvard-Lee area who did not have children enrolled at the branch, and a reception followed the recital. The whole occasion was a very rewarding one that brought increased awareness of this branch's contribution to the area.

The annual meeting 1973 was the first to include the members of the corporation who had contributed to the School during the past year in accordance with the criteria for the recently created friends membership. A sizeable group was present, and Miss Humel gave a special welcome to the new members. In her president's report, she stated that the 1972-73 year had been one of careful planning and re-examination of the Settlement's purposes. There had been a rededication to these purposes as well as renewed effort by countless individuals. Many new procedures had been inaugurated to support existing programs, to create new ones, to give assistance to other agencies and new segments of the community, and to generate as much self help as possible. The responsibility for implementing the various projects was often shared by both the trustees and staff members.

New funds added this year within the memorial scholarship endowment fund included the names of Charlotte A. Ackerman, Irving O. Gressle, Meral Komor, Cleo McNelly, George Anna Meade, and George Szell; honored by contributions made in their names to the tribute scholarship endowment fund were Richard Kauffman, Nellie L. Schreiner, Elizabeth M. Treuhaft, and Howard Whittaker. In addition to these recent funds within the special endowments, friends and trustees established three major funds: The Carl and Caroline Benner Scholarship Fund, The Ann and James C. Brooks, Jr., Scholarship Fund, and the South Side Branch Endowment Fund.

In his annual report to the membership, Howard Whittaker observed that reaching as many people in the community as possible was the guiding principle for all activities. He said that the Settlement was now serving approximately five thousand persons. In accordance with this principle and during the second year of Miss Humel's term as president, a new concept for extended service to the community was introduced. At a meeting in July 1973 of the new visiting committee (composed basically of representatives of other institutions serving as Settlement advisory trustees), with Walter Blodgett, chairman, the proposal was advanced that the Settlement should extend its services to older people and recent retirees. It was the consensus of the committee that because of earlier retirement and the fact that life expectancy had been lengthened, there was a pressing need to serve adults. Something positive, such as private lessons and group music appreciation, should be offered by the School for this age group. Programs could be sent to homes for the elderly and could serve a dual purpose, as they would provide valuable opportunities for performance to advanced students.

Howard Whittaker was fully in accord with the idea, and when the program was announced in the newspapers, he was quoted, "The main thrust in the 1970s will be toward adults." *The Plain Dealer* (January 13, 1974) headlined a notice by saying, "Programs of Note are about to Debut," and went on to say, "The 62-year-old Settlement has taken two big steps for seniors. It has set up special classes for them, and it has programs ready to go out on the road to senior centers, nursing homes, and housing estates." The response by the adult population was extremely favorable, almost overwhelming; this proved the demand for such services and highlighted how well the School was attuned to the needs of the times. These new classes and programs, like music therapy, were a great addition to the Settlement's outreach to the community.

The perspicacity of the visiting committee was inherent in its suggestion that a dean be appointed. Such a position had been unfilled since the resignation of Walter Logan in 1920. Now, with the large enrollment and a faculty of over two hundred, it was impossible for the executive director to have contact with all the faculty or to attend every student recital. A cohesive factor was definitely needed, and a request was made to The Cleveland Foundation for a three-year grant to engage a dean on a part-time basis. The money being granted, Walter Blodgett was named to the deanship. An advisory trustee of the Settlement, a distinguished organist and choir director, Mr. Blodgett had been for many years the curator of musical arts at The Cleveland Museum of Art. About to retire from that position, he was well qualified for the new post at the Settlement. It was expected that the new dean would counsel students in regard to college entrance and scholarships; establish faculty committees for the awarding of scholarships and certificates; aid in filling key faculty positions; assist in periodic revision of curricula, and would help arrange faculty and student recitals as well as master classes. With such a job description, Mr. Blodgett would provide the coordinating element for the School's personnel and services.

Also in July of 1973, the trustees approved the idea of including as honorary members for life those who contributed a minimum of five thousand dollars, an amount which could be cumulative. They also agreed that this same sum be used as the criterion for the establishment of a named scholarship fund, a policy that had been in effect but not formally enacted.

Since the 1973-74 year was the tenth anniversary of the South Side Branch, several special occasions were planned to celebrate this event. Among them was a Christmas program at which a Steinway grand piano, acquired through a grant from the Kulas Foundation, was dedicated; the program was followed by a party for students, parents, and faculty. In order to designate more clearly to the public the area served by the South Side Branch, the board approved, in December 1973, the change in name to Harvard East Branch.

The idea for a program which would grant a degree in music therapy was becoming a reality in 1974. This was to be accomplished through a consortium of colleges and universities with the Settlement as the sponsoring institution. Because of the public's interest in music therapy and that of students entering this field, Baldwin-Wallace College, Case Western Reserve University, Cleveland State University, College of Wooster, Oberlin College, and Ursuline

College had wished for some time to offer degrees in music therapy. However, none of these institutions could provide the necessary practical or laboratory courses. By having the Settlement's services available to them through courses in music therapy training, the granting of degrees would be possible. If a grant from the United States department of health, education, and welfare were forthcoming, this consortium could be launched. An application for such a grant was sent to HEW; at the annual meeting in May 1974 Howard Whittaker reported that HEW had advised him to proceed in a search for a director of this project, even though the approval for the funding might not come until the following spring. The music therapy program was ready to take a large step forward.

Parking problems had plagued the Settlement for a long time. A number of plans had been proposed to solve the situation, but all had to be discarded. Thus it was that in 1974, when University Circle, Inc., offered to sell the School a property on Mistletoe Drive diagonally across from the main building, a solution was proposed — the house on this property might be razed and the space used for parking. The trustees agreed unanimously to accept this practical answer to the problem. Fortunately, several years before this, through the help of trustee Mrs. Dudley S. Blossom, Jr., the William Bingham Foundation had made a grant of fifty thousand dollars to the Settlement for a landscaping program to include additional parking spaces; the money, then, was available.

Early in the same year of 1974, the board of trustees adopted a resolution of memorial tribute to Mrs. Emily McCallip Adler, an honorary trustee who had been director of the Settlement from 1933 to 1945. These had been very challenging years for the School, from depression to war, encompassing also the move from East 93rd Street to Magnolia Drive. Upon leaving the Settlement, Mrs. Adler became director of the Neighborhood Music School in New Haven, Connecticut; she was also active in promoting the National Guild of Community Music Schools and traveled extensively throughout the country for this purpose. A copy of the memorial resolution was sent to Mrs. Adler's sister, Mrs. Mabel McCallip Paul, and shortly thereafter Mrs. Paul created the Emily McCallip Adler Fund within the memorial scholarship endowment.

In March of 1974, two board members and the new dean were honored with Cleveland Arts Prizes given by the Women's City Club: trustee Richard Fleischman was awarded the Cleveland Arts

Prize in Architecture; special citations were given to Alexander C. Robinson, III, honorary trustee, and Dean Walter Blodgett.

In April of 1974, Herbert Elwell, the distinguished composer and music critic who had been a good friend of the Settlement and a member of its faculty, passed away. Through the generosity of Mr. Elwell's family, *The Plain Dealer,* and his friends, the Herbert Elwell memorial scholarship fund was established.

During the year, much work was done by members of the executive committee in updating the contract forms and the personnel practices manual. The revised documents were approved by the board of trustees as was also the executive committee's other recommendation that a scholarship committee be created.

Musical highlights of the 1973-74 school year were master classes given by the distinguished pianist Rudolf Firkusny and Benita Valente, soprano. The world premiere of Howard Whittaker's *Cello Sonatine* was performed by Stephen Geber, principal cellist of The Cleveland Orchestra, and his wife, Judith, a pianist and member of the Settlement faculty. A great coup for the School in April was the winning of the 1974 Metropolitan Opera National Auditions — the most important competition for singers in the United States — by a former student, Alma Jean Smith. She had received her first vocal, piano, and theory training as a scholarship student at the Settlement. As the victor after competing against fifteen hundred entrants, Miss Smith was awarded a contract with the Metropolitan Opera Association.

In May, The Junior League of Cleveland, Inc., opened a house across the street from the School as its Decorators Showhouse, an annual benefit to raise monies for the League's community projects. The women's council of the Settlement seized this opportunity to add to the School's income by serving luncheons for visitors to the League's house. Aside from its fund-raising value, the impact of this project lay in the demonstrated ability of the women's council to respond to an opportune moment to present a promotional interpretation of the Settlement to many new people, and to develop an esprit between council members and the School's personnel. Chessie Systems (formerly Chesapeake and Ohio Railroad Company), a long-standing friend of the School through Howard Skidmore, a trustee, aided the project by printing the brochures which were given to the luncheon guests at the School.

Also in May of 1974, a large recognition party honoring the entire faculties and staffs of the Settlement, its Harvard East Branch and two affiliates, Rainey Institute and the Koch School of Music, was given by the trustees in the Napoleon Room of The Western Reserve Historical Society. Thirty-three persons who had served for ten years or more were given gifts. The three with the longest tenure were also presented special citations for dedicated and exceptional service — Margarita Jolles, for thirty-three years, Margaret Sharp, for thirty-six, and Hyman Schandler for fifty-six.

Born in Russia, Miss Jolles was a teacher of piano, first in her native country, then Germany, and finally the United States. In 1941, the year after her arrival, she became a member of the Settlement's faculty, continuing on as one of its most distinguished members. In 1951, she was appointed associate head of the piano department and served with distinction in this position. Miss Sharp joined the Settlement faculty in 1938 as a teacher of piano. She performed both as pianist and cellist in numerous faculty recitals and in other concerts throughout the Greater Cleveland area. In 1953, she was appointed registrar, and literally thousands of students owe a deep debt of gratitude to her for advice, encouragement, and assistance in many difficult situations. Mr. Schandler, a member of The Cleveland Orchestra since 1927, with many years as principal of the second violin section, came to the Settlement for instruction in 1912, the year it opened, and became a student teacher in 1918. Thus, he had the most extensive teaching career of any faculty member and the longest participation in faculty recitals. As a conductor he founded the Cleveland Women's Orchestra in 1935 which provided valuable experiences for many of the School's students and afforded opportunities for solo performance to young artists. Mr. Schandler's dedication to the Settlement and his contributions to the cultural life of the city through the Women's Orchestra benefited the School in many ways.

The recognition party was a very warm and beautiful occasion for all who attended and was particularly appreciated by the faculty and staff members. At the conclusion of the ceremony, Miss Humel, the president, stated that it was as much an honor for the School as it was for the honored guests to have their service recognized.

At the annual meeting of the corporation's members in May 1974, the president announced the addition of the following to the Honor Roll of Major Contributors during the past year. Mrs. William O. Frohring, The Hankins Foundation, The Thomas F. Peterson

Foundation, Union Commerce Bank, and Mr. and Mrs. Justin G. Zverina. Belatedly, the names of Mr. and Mrs. Francis E. Drury were also added — in the writing of the history, it was discovered that they had been very generous contributors in the early years. Miss Humel also reported the addition of three major scholarship funds: the Harriet S. Eells Memorial Scholarship Fund for black students of voice (established by Mrs. Warren H. Corning in memory of her sister, a former trustee); the George Szell Memorial Scholarship Fund for students of stringed instruments, and The Herbert Elwell Memorial Scholarship Fund, as already mentioned, for students of composition. Within the memorial scholarship endowment, Miss Humel stated that funds were created in the names of Barbara Ellen Adelstein and Margaret Allen Ireland, in addition to those of Emily McCallip Adler and Dora Rucker Meade noted previously. Also, contributions for new funds within the tribute scholarship endowment were received in honor of James Barrett and Dr. Lester G. Glick.

During the two-year presidency of Miss Dorothy Humel, the number of new endowment funds secured was impressive; of great importance was the establishment of the first endowment fund for the Harvard East Branch (originally The South Side Endowment Fund) to be used for general operating purposes; five major scholarship funds were added, as well as eight separate funds within the memorial scholarship endowment and seven within the tribute scholarship endowment. There were eight new names added to the honor roll of major contributors. The complete listing in chronological order of the honor roll and the special funds, trusts, and awards as of May 31, 1974, was as follows:

HONOR ROLL OF MAJOR CONTRIBUTORS

Mr. and Mrs. Francis E. Drury
Mr. and Mrs. Edmund S. Burke, Jr.
Mr. and Mrs. Elroy J. Kulas
Mrs. Dudley S. Blossom, Sr.
Kulas Foundation
The Cleveland Foundation
Mr. and Mrs. Dudley S. Blossom, Jr.
The Louis D. Beaumont Foundation
Mrs. Nettie H. Cook
The George C. and Marion S. Gordon Fund
The Leonard C. Hanna, Jr., Final Fund

Mr. and Mrs. Clarence L. Collens
Mrs. Edwin S. Griffiths
The Louise H. and David S. Ingalls Foundation, Inc.
Mrs. Aber D. Unger
Mr. and Mrs. Willard W. Brown
Mr. and Mrs. Robert H. Gries
Anonymous
Martha Holden Jennings Foundation
Mr. and Mrs. Theo Moll
The William Bingham Foundation
J. F. Lincoln Family Foundation
Mr. and Mrs. Frank K. Griesinger
The George Gund Foundation
Anonymous
Mr. and Mrs. Justin G. Zverina
Mrs. William O. Frohring
The Hankins Foundation
The Thomas F. Peterson Foundation
Union Commerce Bank

SPECIAL FUNDS, TRUSTS, AND AWARDS
The Fynette H. Kulas Fund (1941)
The Settlement Endowment Fund (1959)
The Josef Gingold Violin Scholarship (1960)
The Nathan Fryer Memorial Fund (1961)
The Charles V. Rychlik Memorial Fund (1961)
The Mrs. Sterling Newell Fund (1963)
The Winifred Fryer Memorial Fund (1963)
The Nettie H. Cook Trust (1965)
The Aberd D. Unger Memorial Scholarships (1966)
The Margaret Rusk Griffiths Trust (1968)
The Nellie E. Hinds Memorial Scholarships (1971)
The Marie R. and Raleigh F. Andrie Memorial Fund (1971)
The Harvard East Branch Endowment Fund (1972)
The Carl and Caroline Benner Scholarship Fund (1973)
The Ann and James C. Brooks, Jr. Scholarship Fund (1973)
The Harriet S. Eells Memorial Scholarship Fund (1973)
The George Szell Memorial Scholarship Fund (1974)
The Herbert Elwell Memorial Scholarship Fund (1974)

MEMORIAL SCHOLARSHIP ENDOWMENT FUND
Charlotte A. Ackerman
Barbara Ellen Adelstein
Emily McCallip Adler
Irving O. Gressle
Dr. Jerome Gross
Margaret Allen Ireland
Philip Kirchner
Meral Komor
Justin W. Macklin
Cleo McNelly
Dora Rucker Meade
George Anna Meade
Marjory W. Robinson

TRIBUTE SCHOLARSHIP ENDOWMENT FUND
James Barrett
Edward W. Garfield
Dr. Lester G. Glick
Richard Kauffman
Louis Lane
Nellie L. Schreiner
Elizabeth M. Treuhaft
Howard Whittaker

As a gesture in completing her presidency, Miss Humel presented to Howard Whittaker an album containing the pictures of the past presidents of the board of trustees. This together with the history would provide an important record for the School.

At the annual meeting of the trustees, which immediately followed that of the members, Mrs. Scott R. York was elected to succeed Miss Humel, and, in taking over the presidency, she enumerated the contributions that her predecessor had made to the Settlement during her term of office. Mrs. York mentioned Miss Humel's dedication to and perfectionism in her duties; her talent for raising funds (a substantial amount had been added to the endowment during her presidency), and the recently established membership drive which had brought many new and generous annual contributors to the School; her vision in seeing the need for and her assistance in bringing into being a women's council, the Teens-in-Training program, the

University Circle Center for Community Programs, and the position of dean; and lastly, her awareness of the faculty's contribution to the School which culminated in the recognition party heretofore mentioned. Miss Humel was presented a gold charm bearing the School's new emblem in appreciation of her accomplishments.

This history of the Settlement concludes with the 1974 annual meeting. It is of interest, therefore, to note some of the outstanding faculty who have been a part of the School over the years, and also what some of the students have accomplished. The listing is certainly not comprehensive, merely a representation of the School's quality of music education; it is alphabetical, not chronological.

Outstanding faculty have included Julius Baker, Harold Berkley, Daniel Bonade, Louis Davidson, Rafael Druian, Severin Eisenberger, Herbert Elwell, Felix Eyle, Nathan Fryer, Burton Garlinghouse, Josef Gingold, Maurice Goldman, Boris Goldovsky, George Goslee, Philip Kirchner, Andrius Kuprevicius, Theodore Lettvin, Walter Logan, Daniel Majeske, Martin Morris, Thomas Nyfenger, Theodore Rautenberg, Robert Ripley, Lila Robeson, Leonard Rose, Maurice Sharp, Leonard Shure, Ernst Silberstein, Arnold Steinhardt, William Stokking, and Pauline Thesmacher.

STUDENTS	ACCOMPLISHMENTS
Bernard Adelstein, trumpeter	Principal trumpet, The Cleveland Orchestra
Daniel Barber,	Contestant, Tchaikovsky Piano Competition, Moscow (1974)
Louis Berman, violist and violinist	Former member, The Cleveland Orchestra; teacher in Philadelphia
William Berman, violist	Former member, The Cleveland Orchestra; member, symphony orchestra of Wellington, New Zealand
Muriel Carmen, violist	Member, The Cleveland Orchestra
Roger Drinkall, cellist	Concert artist performing with wife as Drinkall Duo
Zoe Erisman, pianist	Teacher, University of Texas and concert artist
Harold Fink, pianist and composer	Head of music department, Lake Erie College

Michael Flaksman, cellist	Concert artist in Europe
Samuel Goldblum, violist	Former members, The Cleveland Orchestra
William Goldenberg, composer	Composer for movies in Hollywood
Vincent Greicius, violinist	Member, the Metropolitan Opera Orchestra
Dr. Jerome Gross, violinist	Surgeon; concert artist
Margaret Hauptmann, soprano	Concert artist; teacher, Drake University
Randall Hodgkinson, pianist	Concert artist
Gerald Humel, composer and flutist	Fellowship and award-winning composer residing in Berlin
Jon Humphrey, tenor	Concert artist
Penelope Jensen, soprano	Concert artist
Joseph Koch, violinist	Member, The Cleveland Orchestra
Jaime Laredo, violinist	Winner, Queen Elisabeth International Music Competition (of Belgium); international concert artist
Vincenzo Manno, tenor	Concert artist; opera singer in Italy
Seth McCoy, tenor	International concert artist; opera and oratorio singer
Gordon Moebius, pianist	Faculty member, Capital University
Muriel Moebius, violinist	Member, St. Louis Symphony
William Nabors, pianist	Concert artist in Europe
Daisy Newman, soprano	Concert artist
Kenneth Patti, violinist	Former member, The Cleveland Orchestra
John Pavey, bassoonist	Teacher, Eastman School of Music
Edward Payne, tenor	Concert artist in Italy; member, Goldovsky Touring Opera Company
Margaret Pettengill, contralto	Opera singer in Germany
Ronald Phillips, bassoonist	Former member, The Cleveland Orchestra

Donald Plesnicar, oboist	Member, The New Jersey Symphony
Melvin Ritter, violinist	Concert artist; former Concertmaster, St. Louis Symphony
Jerome Rosen, violinist	Member, Boston Symphony Orchestra
Fred Rosenberg, violist	Former member, The Cleveland Orchestra; teacher in Youngstown
Harry Sargous, oboist	Principal, Toronto Symphony
Hyman Schandler, violinist and conductor	Principal, second violin section of The Cleveland Orchestra; conductor, the Cleveland Women's Orchestra
Edward Seferian, violinist and conductor	Conductor, Tacoma Symphony Orchestra
Joseph Senyak, violinist and violist	Former member, The Cleveland Orchestra
Ben Silverberg, violinist	Former assistant concertmaster, The Cleveland Orchestra
Carol Sindell, violinist	Concert artist; teacher at Baldwin-Wallace College; artist in residence at the Wisconsin Conservatory of Music
Alma Jean Smith, soprano	Winner, 1974 Metropolitan Opera National Auditions; member, Metropolitan Opera Association
Anthony Sophos, cellist	Member, New York Philharmonic
Wayne Williams, tenor	Concert artist in Europe
Richard Wilson, composer pianist, teacher	Professor of Music, Vassar College
Harvey Wolfe, cellist	Member, The Cleveland Orchestra
Martin Zielinski, trumpeter	Teacher, University of Akron
Robert Zupnik, oboist	Member, The Cleveland Orchestra

Epilogue: What's Past Is Prologue

IN RECORDING THESE SIXTY YEARS and more, perhaps the account has seemed to lean towards the sundial view, the record of only the brighter hours. However, mention has been made of the years of the depression, of the financial difficulties when the reach of the School exceeded its means, as well as other challenges. No institution is without peaks and vales, but it is evident that The Cleveland Music School Settlement has had an unprecedented development and can claim a notable record of accomplishment. It has become a sophisticated and excellent institution of national stature, one which many regard as pre-eminent among community music schools in the United States. Its emphasis has been not only on talent specifically, but on broader purposes to nurture the love of music and to provide opportunities for the humblest citizen to enjoy and study good music. Therein has been its strength.

What of the future? In this epoch of mankind's history, there is no Delphic oracle to consult. If there were, perhaps in answer to the question, "What must be done to ensure a bright future for the School?" — the answer might be the words Pindar used in his second Pythian Ode for Hieron of Syracuse: "Become what you are." The reply is ambiguous, as were all the prognostications of the oracle, the course of action to be taken dependent upon the interpretation of the answer. If taken literally, and no changes were ever made, failure would ensue. If it were to be construed as keeping an open mind, being sensitive and adaptable to changing needs — as the trustees and faculty have been in the past — then the School will continue to flourish. That it was ahead of the times from the very beginning is evident from what the last self-study said:

> This institution has always been closely attuned to the needs of the community, and it must necessarily be flexible and respond to situations as they arise. Finally, The Cleveland Music School Settlement is dedicated to the continual search for the best ways to serve the Greater Cleveland community in bringing together persons of different racial,

religious, and economic backgrounds. It has been demonstrated to us time and time again that a most powerful force to achieve this is through the media of the arts.

With such a statement, the School's future is assured.

APPENDIX I

ENROLLMENT STATISTICS (1969-1970)

INCOME	LOWER $7,000 AND LESS	LOWER MIDDLE $7,000-$11,000	MIDDLE $11,000-$15,000	$18,000 AND OVER
Main School	33	26	23	18
West Side Branch	16	82	2	0
South Side Branch	10	90	0	0
Extension Program	100	0	0	0
Rainey Institute	87	13	0	0

	ANGLO-SAXON	EAST EUROPEAN	SOUTH EUROPEAN	BLACK	ORIENTAL
Main School	30	21	10	38	1
West Side Branch	29	54	11	4	2
South Side Branch	10	0	0	90	0
Extension Program	21	30	10	39	0
Rainey Institute	3	7	0	90	0

APPENDIX II

PRESIDENTS OF THE CLEVELAND MUSIC SCHOOL SETTLEMENT

Albert Reese Davis	1912-1913
Edward A. Foote	1913-1915
Mrs. George N. Sherwin	1915-1916
Mrs. Otis Southworth	1916-1919
Frank Muhlhauser	1919-1921
Mrs. Francis E. Drury	1921-1923
Arthur Pomeroy	1923-1926
Mrs. Clarence L. Collens	1926-1929
Mrs. Frank E. House	1929-1931
Edward W. Garfield	1931-1956
Edward F. Meyers	1956-1958
Alexander C. Robinson, III	1958-1962
Dr. Lester G. Glick	1962-1966
Mrs. Webb Chamberlain	1966-1968
Charles Klaus	1968-1970
Richard S. Cole	1970-1972
Mrs. Dorothy Humel Hovorka	1972-1974
Mrs. Scott R. York	1974-1976
Donald M. Gossard	1976-1978
Dr. Lester G. Glick	1978-1980
Allan J. Zambie	1980-1982
Mrs. J. Heywood Alexander	1982-1985
B. Scott Isquick	1985-1987
Mrs. Carlton B. Schnell	1987-

DIRECTORS OF THE CLEVELAND MUSIC SCHOOL SETTLEMENT

Miss Linda W. Sampson	1912-1918
Mrs. Catherine E. Saunders	1918-1931
Mrs. Martha Cruikshank Ramsey	1931-1933
Mrs. Emily McCallip Adler	1933-1945
Miss Louise Palmer Walker	1945-1947
Howard Whittaker	1948-1984
Malcolm J. Tait	1984-1986
Miss Linda Allen, *acting director*	1986-1988
David R. Pierce	1988-

About the Author:

Silvia Wunderlich Zverina

S HE WAS BORN Silvia Alcina Wunderlich in England of American parents on June 3, 1903. Avidly interested in ballet as a young child, she was awarded a certificate of merit for her dancing, one of the judges being Anna Pavlova; later she won first prize in this same competition which was held in London to raise money for charity.

In 1912 the Wunderlich family moved to the United States. In her early teens, Silvia entered the *St. Nicholas Magazine* Writing Contest several times and was awarded both silver and gold medals. While at Cleveland's East High School, she won first prize in the Christmas Story Contest sponsored by the *Cleveland Plain Dealer* and also took the leading role in the senior class play.

After graduating from Flora Stone Mather College of Western Reserve University in 1925, she began her professional career as secretary to Frederic Allen Whiting, the first director of The Cleveland Museum of Art. Her interest in art took her to Athens, Greece, for study at The American School of Classical Studies, after which she received the M.A. degree in 1936 from what is now Case Western Reserve University. During her twenty-eight years as a staff member of The Cleveland Museum of Art, she attained the curatorship of Greek and Roman Art, was also in charge of the Egyptian collection, and was editor of the Museum's bulletin.

Silvia Wunderlich Zverina is a member of the Art Museum's Advisory Council and served two terms as its co-chairman; she is also an honorary member of the Museum's Women's Council. A past trustee and president of Phil Beta Kappa Cleveland Association, she is also a past member of The Cleveland Astronomical Society's executive board and was the Society's librarian for seventeen years. Mrs. Zverina holds a life membership in The Textile Arts Club and is a trustee of The Cleveland Institute of Art and The Cleveland Music School Settlement.

Index

Colophon

And They Shall Have Music, the History of
The Cleveland Music School Settlement
has been published in an edition of
fifteen hundred copies by
The Cobham and Hatherton Press
of Cleveland, Ohio
on Mohawk Superfine paper
in September 1988.